Following the Footsteps of the Invisible

CISTERCIAN STUDIES SERIES NUMBER TWO HUNDRED THIRTY-NINE

Following the Footsteps of the Invisible

The Complete Works of Diadochus of Photikē

Introduction, Translation, and Notes by

Cliff Ermatinger

α

Cistercian Publications
www.cistercianpublications.org

LITURGICAL PRESS
Collegeville, Minnesota
www.litpress.org

A Cistercian Publications title published by Liturgical Press

Cistercian Publications
Editorial Offices
Abbey of Gethsemani
3642 Monks Road
Trappist, Kentucky 40051
www.cistercianpublications.org

1   2   3   4   5   6   7   8   9

Library of Congress Cataloging-in-Publication Data

Diadochus, Bishop of Photice, 5th cent.
    [Works. English. 2010]
    Following the footsteps of the invisible : the complete works of Diadochus of Photike / [translated by] Cliff Ermatinger.
        p.   cm. — (Cistercian studies series ; no. 239)
    "Cistercian Publications."
    Includes bibliographical references (p.   ) and index.
    ISBN 978-0-87907-239-1 — ISBN 978-0-87907-928-4 (e-book)
    1. Theology.   I. Ermatinger, Cliff.   II. Title.   III. Series.

BR65.D375E5 2010
230'.19—dc22
                                                        2010017268

To Archbishop Jerome Listecki—

with gratitude.

Contents

Acknowledgments

Special thanks to Beth Hanan who, amid raising a family and the demands of her trial work as an attorney, was very generous with her time proofreading the text. Everyone should have a sister like Beth.

Introduction to the Life and Spirituality of Diadochus of Photikē

Draw me in your footsteps, let us run together[1]

Diadochus of Photikē

A fifth-century mystic perceived his hidden Lover's approach. He let God enrapture his heart once and for all and dedicated the rest of his life to following the footsteps of the Invisible One.

Although our author is the most important ascetical writer of his century, solid data on him is quite scarce. He lived sometime between 400 and 487 as bishop of Photikē in Old Epiros—a place besieged by invasions, covered over by earthquakes, and eventually lost for a while to history until some excavations in northeastern Greece turned up evidence of its location at the end of the nineteenth century.[2] Although Photius says otherwise,[3] Diadochus's name does not appear on any of the documents of the Council of Chalcedon (451), therefore his episcopal ordination

---

[1] Song 1:4.
[2] See Demetrios Triantaphyllopoulos, "He mesaionike Photikē kai he these tes sten Palai Epeiro," *Actes du Xe Congrés International d´Archéologie Chrétienne* 2, 1984, 577–85.
[3] PG 103:1089–1192.

1

must have been posterior to the council. Since his signature does appear along with the names of the other bishops of Old Epiros at the bottom of a letter to Emperor Leo (457) reporting the murder of Bishop Proterius of Alexandria as a result of some theological differences with some Monophysites, his episcopal ordination was conferred between those years.

It seems Diadochus's turbulent times not only brought about his early death but also served to broaden his influence on other spiritual leaders. If there is any truth to the theory[4] that Diadochus was pirated off to North Africa during a Vandal foray through Epiros, then that would explain how he came to be the spiritual father to Eugene, bishop of far-off Carthage, and to the ascetical writer Julian Pomerius, as the African bishop Victor of Vita says. Of the "great" Diadochus he also says that he "merits every sort of praise since his many writings illumine the Catholic faith like bright stars."[5]

Although heaven gained a martyr, the church lost a shepherd and spiritual giant. Of "his many writings" only four have survived and his authorship of one of them is disputed. Taken in strict terms, Victor seems to speak of dogmatic treatises. Of the four works, the three briefer writings are clearly dogmatic, while Diadochus's masterpiece *Discourses on Judgment and Spiritual Discernment* (which Diadochus also calls *One Hundred Gnostic Chapters*) today would be relegated to the genre of spiritual theology. Nonetheless, our author would resist such a distinction, since for him it is precisely by living the life of prayer and asceticism proposed in his *Discourses* that one is equipped to utter correctly a word about theology. The only authentic theology is

---

[4] Henri Irenee Marou, "Diadoque de Photicé et Victor de Vita," *Christiana Tempora*, 373–80, Rome, 1978; also, Angelo Cardinal Mai brought this fact to light in 1840, see PG 65:1139–40.

[5] Edouárd Des Places, SJ, ed. and trans., *Diadoque de Photicé: Oeuvres spirituelle*, SCh 5bis (Paris: Du Cerf, Paris, 1955), 9. This is the critical edition of the Greek text used for this English translation.

lived theology, for "nothing is more miserable than a Godless mind philosophising about God."[6]

His Works

In Diadochus of Photikē we find a pure Greek specimen. Even as Greece was busy hellenizing the East, its own culture was undergoing latinization from the West. The price of exportation was unintended imports. This is clear to readers of Greek works of that era. The Attic Peninsula seemed to be undergoing an identity crisis that brought with it social, religious, and linguistic syncretism—all of which our author managed to resist. Since the overall level of Greek had deteriorated and writers of the fifth century became increasingly aware of how far their language had drifted from the beauty of Classical Greek (they had lost the use of the optative, for example) many writers clumsily attempted to rectify this. Others simply kept on writing as the linguistically mixed masses spoke. If we could imagine a large portion of our immigrant population speaking English as a second language, some of whom throw in a few "forsooths" every now and then in memory of past linguistic glory, and suddenly someone were to appear writing with the purity of style of John Donne, we might get a clearer picture of Diadochus's cultural stature. As the beauty of his language attracted many more adepts it also proved to be a worthy platform for his solid doctrine. He set a new standard for subsequent generations.

The *Discourses on Judgment and Spiritual Discernment* is by far Diadochus's most famous and influential work. The critical edition of the Greek text offers the primary title *One Hundred Gnostic Chapters*, which is followed by a decalogue of the life of Christian virtue. A secondary title follows on the heels of these definitions and this is the title I have chosen to use. Nonetheless, Diadochus

---

[6] Gnostic Chapter 7 (hereafter, references made to this work will be identified by GC).

seems to offer yet another title as an afterthought, calling it his *Ascetical Treatises* on the last page. Each title is fitting.

A collection of one hundred brief sayings or "chapters," known as a "century," was a popular literary device among spiritual writers of the ancient world. The number one hundred points toward perfection, a reflection of God in his unicity and multiplicity. It may have been Evagrius Pontus (345–392), who introduced this practice into Christian literature with his own *Gnostic Chapters*. Century writers began to spring up throughout the Middle East and Greece over the next few hundred years. After Evagrius, the most important among the proponents of this literary form are chronologically Mark the Hermit, Diadochus of Photikē, and Maximus the Confessor. Sometimes a century was a collection of sayings, more often these maxims regarded a particular area of the spiritual life redacted by a spiritual father for his disciples. The disciples would memorize the one maxim at the beginning of the day and spend the rest of the day interiorizing that thought amid their tasks and times of quiet.

It should be mentioned that Diadochus has his own style of century. Rather than offer weighty, challenging aphorisms, his chapters, with their multiple ideas, offer much more in one chapter than other century writers. He makes his point and then, having gotten the reader's attention, uses the opportunity to engage his theological foes. Other times he uses colorful metaphors to exemplify his rules for discernment. But all that he says remains on the level of experiential theology and is quite practical.

The ten definitions with which Diadochus begins this work set the foundation for everything he is about to say. It seems that such distinctions are not only necessary to understand our author's usage but also offer us a glimpse into his spiritual experience. A large portion of the *Gnostic Chapters* offers insightful rules of discernment (*diakrisis* in Greek—a term that means to distinguish, separate, cut), and this seems to be the methodology of the Diadochan corpus. He wants to define terminology, distinguish the provenance of the interior movements that accompany the spiritual life, guide the spiritually perplexed to the heights of divine union, and separate orthodox teaching from the dominant heresies of his age.

The Homily on the Ascension of Our Lord Jesus Christ is similar to his *Gnostic Chapters* in its elevated and rhythmic Greek style and its elongated phrases that can give headaches to translators. The *Homily* has the clear purpose of defending Christ's divinity and human natures and he carries this out masterfully. In it he makes the crowning victory of the Incarnation the divinization of man. His finale is a christological confession meant to trump the Monophysites.

The Vision is a communication with Saint John the Baptist in the guise of a dream. Using an effective question-answer format, Diadochus's inquiries regarding contemplation, the beatific vision, apparitions, and angels are all satisfied. In some regard aspects of his teaching resemble Pseudo-Dionysius's angelology. No manuscript of *The Vision* prior to the thirteenth century exists and the eleven existing texts all attribute this work to the bishop of Photikē.

The Catechesis is an enigma. Although it follows the same question-answer format as *The Vision*, some have attributed its authorship to Simeon the New Theologian. Nonetheless, it is absent from lists of Simeon's works and most recent scholarship seems unwilling to attribute it to Simeon. This work considers God's relationship to the world, the divine attributes, and angelology, ending with a reminder of the role of good works in the order of salvation. Regardless of doubts that some scholars have in ascribing this work to Diadochus, Des Places includes it in his critical edition and so have I.

Diadochus's Milieu

We can only understand Diadochus if we consider his context. The century he was born into was fraught with theological and political disputes, and the serious Christian was pulled in different directions by opposing schools of spirituality. The two dominant currents of mystical theology of the day were, on the one hand, intellectualist or philosophical, and, on the other, aesthetic or biblical.

The earliest Christian writers, beginning with Saint Paul, provided the foundation for the aesthetic school, which emphasized the role of the will and the affections in the order of loving communication with God. Macarius, a contemporary of Diadochus, was the most influential proponent of this school in its orthodox form. Messalianism was a heterodox expression of this school.

On the other hand, the intellectualist school stressed the role of the intellect (*nous*) in the order of communication with God under the banner of the dictum, "the goal of life is contemplation."[7] This school was founded by Origen and the Alexandrians and was most widely promulgated by Evagrius of Pontus, who immediately preceded and influenced our author.

Although the Messalians on the one side and Origen and Evagrius on the other were condemned by the church, Diadochus reveals traces of both schools in synthetic form, avoiding the exaggerations taught by these schools, proving that they both had much that was salvageable.

Evagrius proposed a Platonic anthropology, holding that material is oriented toward sin and in need of being spiritualized. Although the concept of the heart is important for Evagrius, he makes the term interchangeable with mind or soul, following the Platonists. Diadochus will have none of this. Diadochus proposes a positive anthropology that sees the flesh just as penetrated by grace as the soul is from the moment of baptism. Although Evagrius barely mentions the sacraments, Diadochus's theology is a theology of baptism and its consequences. Further, Diadochus's use of the word "heart" is biblical, implying the entire person as receptor of God's grace. Nonetheless, Diadochus shares much of Evagrius's thought with regard to the insubstantiality of evil, prayer free of all forms and images, the role of dispassion, and types of demons.[8]

The Messalian heresy confused the presence and work of God's grace with "experience" or feelings. Such subjectivity obviously lent itself to error under the guise of "mystical materialism."[9] If

---

[7] Clement of Alexandria, *Stromata*, 2.21.

[8] All of these themes will be taken up later.

[9] Irenee Hausherr, "L'erreur fondamentale et la logique de Messalianisme," *Orientalia Christiana Periodica* 1 (1935): 328–60.

the Pelagians downplayed the effects of original sin and mitigated the need for grace, the Messalians responded with their own aberration claiming that everyone was conceived not only in sin but also in a state of diabolical possession. Further, this dour theology held that sacramental baptism and Eucharist provided no remedy. Such demons can only be expelled through prayer and fasting (Mark 9:29) was their clarion call and, unlike the exceptional case of which our Lord speaks, this was the state of the general, albeit unaware, populace. Thus, the rule of the day was excessive asceticism and constant prayer until such point that the person arrived at the much-awaited experience of liberation from the possessing demon. The continual prayer and asceticism required of Messalians precluded other activities and eventually invited the liberating grace whose advent was accompanied by visible, tangible phenomena, ending with the divinization of the soul.[10]

The great spiritual writer now known as Pseudo-Macarius attempted to correct some of the errors of the Messalian sect. It seems that one of Diadochus's aims was to further correct Pseudo-Macarius. Diadochus retains the notion of unceasing prayer, but not to the exclusion of other responsibilities, since prayer, more than an activity, is an attitude resulting from a relationship. Diadochus also clearly promotes the notion of spiritual progress but recognizes that the Holy Spirit is the foremost protagonist on the journey to spiritual perfection. Further, our author will not deny the efficacy and, indeed, the necessity of prayer and asceticism in the order of salvation and sanctification, but his is a refreshing spirituality which avoids excess of any stripe save in the area of *agapē*.

One of Diadochus's many virtues is his ability to find a middle way amid so many exaggerations. Thus his response was equilibrium with regard to fasting[11] and penance,[12] happiness and

---

[10] Friedrich Dörr, *Diadochus und die Messalianer: ein Kampf zwischen wahrer und falscher Mystiker in fünften Jahrhundert* (Freiburg im Breisgau: Herder & Co., 1937).

[11] See GC 47.

[12] See GC 45.

lamentation,[13] use of alcohol[14] and food,[15] and even prayer.[16] Prayer, sacrifice, moderation, and the life of virtue are necessary to continue on the path of transformation in Diadochus's teaching. Yet they are never the beginning or end of it since love is the fulfillment of the law. God's grace initiates the process in baptism thus making it possible to carry out the above practices. Grace seconded by loving human will brings divinization to completion.

Questions on grace and anthropology could be adequately addressed only in light of a healthy Christology—and there was widespread disparity of teaching in the fifth century. The degree of theological confusion was equaled only by the passion with which it was promoted. No sooner had Nestorius been condemned in his attempt to correct the Arian heresy by postulating two persons and two natures in Christ, than others took up yet another heretical standard, holding that our Lord, as one person, had only one nature. These said that in some way our Lord's human nature had been swallowed up by or absorbed into his divine nature—hence the name "Monophysite." Whereas centuries later Nietzsche would tout "philosophy done with a hammer," the Monophysites preceded him by doing theology with a sword. These are the scholars who killed Bishop Proterius of Alexandria as mentioned above. The Nestorianism of the Antiochians and the Monophysitism of the Alexandrians were condemned at the Council of Chalcedon in 451. Since the condemnation was not enough to quell the confusion, Diadochus joined in the fray.

Diadochus's insight and balance have influenced posterior generations from the sixth to the eighteenth centuries. Maximus the Confessor quotes him several times.[17] Photius sings the praises

---

[13] See GC 68, 69.

[14] See GC 47.

[15] See GC 43-51.

[16] See GC 68.

[17] *Opuscula Theologica et Polemica*, PG 91:277C; *Disputatio cum Phyrro*, PG 91:301C, where he quotes GC 5. And *Quaest. Et respon.*, PG 90:792C, where he quotes GC 100.

of the *Gnostic Chapters* in his Bibliotheca.[18] Both John Climacus
and Mark the Hermit favorably refer to Diadochus. His influence
is perhaps most visible in the writings of Simeon the New Theologian as well as other philokalic writers such as Barsanouphios,
Nicephoros of Athos, Gregory of Palamas, and Nicodemos of the
Holy Mountain as well as the author of *The Way of the Pilgrim*. In
the West, the Society of Jesus recommended that its novice masters
read Diadochus's *Gnostic Chapters* to better fulfill their duties as
spiritual directors.[19] Given some similarities in their respective
rules for discernment of spirits, many have claimed that Ignatius
of Loyola was influenced by our author. This cannot be so since
Ignatius had no knowledge of Greek and it was a Jesuit son of
Ignatius who first translated the *Gnostic Chapters* into Latin late
in the sixteenth century.[20]

Diadochus's Spirituality

Image and Likeness—the Alpha and Omega

In commenting on the creation of the human in Genesis 1:26,
Saint Irenaeus introduces to Christian anthropology the distinction between image and likeness, namely, image (*methexis*) meaning ontological participation and likeness (*mimesis*) reflecting the
proportionate degree of man's moral resemblance to God.[21] For
Tertullian, image is an indelible ontological reality, while likeness
is the *ruah* (see Gen 2:7), the spiritual life of man that, unlike the
image, can indeed be lost.[22] Our author continues this line of
thought albeit with a rather original treatment of the distinction.

Diadochus stands out for his positive vision of the material
world in general and human nature in particular. He takes pains

---

[18] See *Analecta Bollandiana* 81 (1963): 414–17.

[19] "Regulae magistri novitiorum Libri ad usum magistri novitiorum
accomodati," *Institutum Societatis Iesu* 3 (1893): 121.

[20] PG 65:1167–1212.

[21] See *Adv. Haer.* 5.6.1; 5.8.1; 5.16.2.

[22] See *Bapt.* 5.6.7.

to stress the ongoing goodness of creation and the human condition, for God created the human in his image[23] and likeness.[24] The image of God is found in the soul's higher regions,[25] which have become darkened by original sin. The Incarnation provides the solution to this unfortunate state, and its merits begin to work on the soul from the moment of baptism. This "bath of holiness" allows the process of transformation to go forward, but personal fragmentation still needs to be remedied. The reintegration of the scattered parts is the path to the restoration of the lost likeness.

> The other part, which is "in the likeness," he hopes to bring about with our cooperation. When the soul begins to taste the goodness of the Holy Spirit with profound sentiments, then we ought to know that grace is beginning to paint the likeness over the image. In the same way, in fact, that painters first sketch the figure of a man in one color, and then little by little make it flourish with one pigmentation upon another, reflecting even the model's hair faithfully, so too the grace of God first establishes a sketch of "in the image" through baptism as when the human was first created. When grace sees that we desire with all our heart the beauty of the likeness and to be naked and without fear in its workshop, then it makes virtue flourish upon virtue, thus elevating the soul's beauty from glory to glory, it places upon it the distinguishing marks of "the likeness."[26]

"In this way spiritual sense reveals that we have been formed 'in the likeness'; yet it is through illumination that we will know the perfection of likeness."[27] This likeness is a goal to be attained only through human cooperation with grace. Just as the Bride of Christ is adorned by the good deeds of the saints (see Rev 19:8), meaning that the degree of beauty of the church triumphant in

---

[23] "It is in the soul with its intellectual movement that we are in the image of God, and the body is akin to its dwelling place" (GC 79).

[24] See GC 4.

[25] See GC 78.

[26] GC 89.

[27] GC 89.

Heaven is, to some extent, dependent on free human actions accomplished through grace, so too each member's degree of likeness to God is determined by his or her free acts.

The arrival at perfect likeness to God befits the soul destined for divinization (*theosis*) and, ultimately, for mystical matrimony. At this stage the soul is shot through with the light and love of God. "Such a one is present and absent in this life. He has his body for a dwelling place, but vacates it through love. He relentlessly moves toward God in his soul. Once he has transcended his self-love through love for God, his heart becomes consumed in the fire of love and clings to God with unyielding desire."[28]

The consummation of *theosis* occurs in the *eschaton*, when the perfect are permitted to enter into the divine nuptials. Diadochus points to Christ's dual nature as a reference to our destiny. Christ's ascension means that he is taken up into glory (see 1 Tim 3:16) in his human nature in order not to violate the laws of human nature, which explains why the saints will be caught up in the clouds to meet the Lord (see 1 Thess 4:17). "For what is fitting for the Incarnate God's body is also fitting for those he will divinize through the abundance of his grace, because it pleases God to make gods of humans."[29]

Being made god by God, a hallmark of Byzantine theology, means an accidental, as opposed to substantial, participation in God's nature (see 2 Pet 1:4) summed up by the dictum "God became man that we might become gods."[30] This participation—a gift of grace to which God invites each person—is a participation in Christ's humanity, which has been divinized. Becoming divine by participation implies no violence to human nature, rather this transformation is a return to God's original plan for humanity, becoming authentically human and adequate for eternal intimacy with God. "In this way it is a habit, not a nature, that the Incarnation of the Word modified, so that we might be stripped of the memory of evil and robed in the charity of God: not transformed

---

[28] GC 14.
[29] Homily VI.
[30] Athanasius, *De incarnatione*, 54.5.

into what we were not, but renewed through glory by the transformation into what we were."[31]

Personal Fragmentation and Aisthēsis

In their original state our first parents enjoyed utter integrity. Diadochus stresses this fact by pointing to one all-important aspect for his anthropology—*aisthēsis*, the lone sense that oriented the entire person through unmistakable perception of God.[32] After the Fall, the image was retained but likeness suffered effacement, albeit not total obliteration. Further, evidence of this distortion is the interior division we all experience, the disintegration of the one sense into many fragmented parts, all becoming senses in their own right, but damaged and in need of redemption and reintegration back into the one, preternatural sense.

Beyond the interior division, now sadly proper to the human condition, this division directs worldviews and becomes institutionalized. The thirteenth-century intellectual divorce that occurred when theology was shoehorned into philosophical methodology in order to become more "scientific" comes to mind. Among the disastrous results were nominalism, an increase in superstition, and doubt with regard to the intelligibility of God. Centuries before, Diadochus addressed this issue: "It is always better to await the illumination of faith, energized by love, which equips us to speak, since nothing is more miserable than a Godless mind philosophising about God."[33] The key to an integral worldview is an integrated world visionary, and this begins with his own healing. This is played out, to a great extent, in what Diadochus terms the "sense."

Since Diadochus's notion of the sense is central to his anthropology, touched by grace, it becomes a focal point in his experiential theology. Sense then is coupled to practically every part of

[31] Homily VI.
[32] See GC 29.
[33] GC 7.

human makeup in an effort to show how far this fragmentation has gone. Some of his usages of the word "sense" follow:

1. Sense of the heart "enables the *nous* to breathe the perfume of supernatural goods,"[34] and the heart is the personal core of the human person, the root of all human activity and passivity. Heart is located at the deepest center of the soul and even of the *nous*, "where love is transformed into knowledge." The heart has members and even "visible parts"[35] by which Diadochus seems to mean those areas more easily accessible through reflection as opposed to the hidden places where grace resides. These hidden places only become manifest through divine movements there, which arouse the sense.

2. Intellectual sense: by way of the sense, the *nous* progresses and prepares itself to thus receive all the virtues,[36] the highest of which is *agapē*.

3. Corporal senses: they have their corresponding interior senses and, though exterior, they are to be neither shunned nor coddled but ordered. They have a role in "the entire person turn[ing] toward the Lord"[37] and "as a result, grace, by way of the spiritual sense, makes the body rejoice with ineffable exultation in those who advance in knowledge."[38] "And from that moment onward, he comes to find himself immersed in such an ardent longing for the illumination of the intellect, penetrating even his bones."[39] This sense of longing is an anticipation of the glorified body.

4. Interior sense: where the person enjoys union with God through purity.[40]

---

[34] GC 23.
[35] GC 85.
[36] See GC 89.
[37] GC 85.
[38] GC 79.
[39] GC 14.
[40] See GC Def. 8.

5. Deep sense: this is reached toward the end of the spiritual itinerary.[41]

6. "Total sense of fullness": this is a key concept for Diadochus. This is experiential knowledge that involves the entire person (*plērophoria*—"total"). *Plērophoria* also means "certainty." The mystics never doubt the reality of their experience. Once this sense has been satisfied the person will never return to the delights of this passing world.[42] But this total sense of fullness is only tasted by those to whom the Holy Spirit has granted it and is, in part, dependent on the degree of their fervent love.[43]

7. Imperceptible sense: the sanctifying action of the Holy Spirit secretly at work in the recesses of the soul unperceived by the host soul.[44]

Peira—*Experience*

Given that the spirituality of Diadochus is nothing if not a lived theology, it is logical that he places the role of "experience" at center stage. In fact, the word appears on practically every page of his *Gnostic Chapters*.

Although a common term in modern spirituality, aspiration toward an experience of God's grace was also an important facet of certain schools of Byzantine spirituality. Diadochus's nemeses, the Messalians, placed an exaggerated degree of importance on what they termed experience, the sensate awareness of God's action. Regardless of his opposition to the sect, Diadochus used their vocabulary in an orthodox way.

The type of experience to which Diadochus refers can be achieved through prayer and intimate contact with the divine Beloved. Such experiences fill the soul with light that the world

---

[41] See GC 88.
[42] See GC 44.
[43] See GC 90.
[44] See GC 85.

can never offer.[45] Such experiences occur in the sense and result in knowledge. To underline the primacy of the experience of God though prayer Diadochus says, "Spiritual discourse brings the intellectual sense to full measure. It comes from God borne by the power of love. . . . [T]hrough its contemplations it is filled in proportion to the measure of desire in its exercise of charity. It is always better to await the illumination of faith, energized by love."[46]

Diadochus presents a sort of virtuous circle brought about by the experience-sense-knowledge paradigm. The experience of grace serves as a reserve from which the sense can draw and ushers in true knowledge of God, which, in turn, brings about a certain communion between God and the warrior.[47] "Indeed, knowledge unites the human to God by experience."[48] This unifying experience brings about a transformation in the heart of the warrior to such an extent that he or she begins to have God's sentiments and vision, seeing even those who insult and attack him or her as God sees them.[49]

Here it is clear that, for Diadochus, experience is not merely a feeling or something sensed—although it includes that phenomenon. Experience is an awareness of God's love lived out in the sense of the heart which, from there, penetrates the entire person.[50] In those

> who have willingly detached themselves from the goods of this life in hopes of future goods . . . self-mastery makes bodily attractions to die off. In them alone, thanks to their

---

[45] See GC 11.

[46] GC 7.

[47] Diadochus frequently uses the term *agōnistēs* (meaning athlete, wrestler, fighter, combatant, or warrior) to describe the contemplative person who has taken to the path of spiritual perfection. Since he describes the following of Christ in terms of spiritual combat, I have chosen to translate this term as "warrior."

[48] GC 9.

[49] See GC 91.

[50] See GC 14.

detachment, can the mind exercise at full strength so as to perceive God's ineffable blessings. As a result it transmits its own share of joy even to the body, in proportion to its progress, exulting without ceasing in its full confession of love [see Ps 41:5]. "My heart puts its trust in him;" he says; "I have been helped, my flesh has bloomed again, I thank him with all my heart" [Ps 27:7]. The joy that actually is produced in the soul and the body is a reliable reminder of incorruptible life.[51]

In GC 79 Diadochus reiterates how the experience of God's love penetrates, purifies, and delights the *nous*, the sense, and the body. This formula is particular to Diadochus who insists that the *peira* does not occur only in the *nous* but throughout the entire person because grace penetrates the entire person.

Baptismal Grace

The path to reintegration of the senses and restoration of the likeness requires divine intervention through grace and human cooperation with that grace. God's initiative through grace and the human's ability to respond through discernment of spirits form the two poles of Diadochus's spirituality. More than a doctrine, Diadochus's theology presents us with a relationship in process. This process begins at the moment of baptism: "Through the regeneration of baptism holy grace obtains two benefits for us, one of which infinitely surpasses the other. It grants us the first immediately, since we are renewed in the water itself which washes us of every stain of sin and it restores all the etchings of the soul—that is, making evident what is 'in the image'—cleansing it of every stain of sin."[52]

Baptism has profound effects on the soul, one of which is the person's ability to desire what he ought to desire. This is part of the path of reintegration:

---

[51] GC 25.
[52] GC 89.

From the moment of baptism, as I mentioned, grace hides itself in the depths of the spirit, its presence concealed even from our very senses. But when one begins to long for God with total conviction, then in sublime colloquy it communicates a portion of its wealth to the soul through the intellect's senses. From the moment in which he has firmly set his heart upon complete possession of what he has discovered his desire is such that he is happily willing to abandon all of this world's present goods in order truly to acquire the field in which the treasure of this life lies hidden.[53]

Describing grace's effects on the interior life Diadochus calls our attention above all to its operation on the intellect, memory, and *aisthēsis*. Conspicuously absent in Diadochus's spirituality is any emphasis on the will. When treating the post-baptismal state, which does not completely do away with concupiscence, he refers to the "two-way inclination of our desire [or will]" and makes a few passing references to this faculty.[54] The will seems to be a function of the sense, which is not entirely unthinkable if we are to follow the dictum that the will always chooses the good, albeit often merely a subjective good, while the *aisthēsis*, or our perceptive faculty, is also led by attractive goods. Yet in the preternatural state the human's only faculty was the perceptive faculty. While it is the intellect that informs the will, and therefore plays a prominent role in Western thought, for Diadochus, it is the sense that needs to be reeducated in order to recognize and respond to true goods. The primacy of sense underlines Diadochus's entire system of experiential theology, and such perception will be necessary in order successfully to engage in the post-baptismal struggles that must surely ensue.

Thus it was for the soul and the body that the holy Word of God was made flesh and, as God, liberally grants us the water of salvation through the baptism of regeneration. Through the action of the life-giving and Holy Spirit we are regenerated.

[53] GC 77.
[54] See GC 5, 25, 93.

Thus we are purified immediately in body and soul—that is, if one is completely oriented toward God—because the Holy Spirit takes up residence in us and sin is evicted from us. So it is impossible that in the soul's simple and integral form two persons could subsist—as some hold. Since through the baptismal bath divine grace adheres to the lineaments of the image —as a guarantee of likeness—where is the Evil One going to stay, for what partnership do light and darkness have with one another? We who have taken up the course of holy combat believe that through the bath of incorruptibility the multiform serpent is cast out of the treasure chamber of the intellect. Nor should we be surprised if after our baptism, along with good things, we should also think crude things. For the bath of sanctity takes away from us the stain of sin, but it does not change this two-way inclination of our desire, nor does it impede demons from making war against us or speaking deceitful words to us, so that what we, as carnal people are incapable of protecting, do indeed preserve through the power of God insofar as we take up the weapons of righteousness.[55]

Evil and Spiritual Combat

As the waters of baptism pour the Holy Spirit's presence into the soul, the diabolical occupant of the previously unwashed soul is necessarily evicted to the outer regions of the person. He continues his work albeit from a different vantage point and with less efficacy.

Evil, for Diadochus, is a nonentity. Nonetheless, in a diabolical perversion of creation, disobedient choices lend evil substance: "Evil is not in nature nor is anyone evil by nature, since God made nothing evil [see Gen 1:31]. But when in the concupiscence of heart someone gives shape to that which is not in reality, then precisely that which he desires begins to exist."[56] The ensuing schizophrenia of sin leaves the person broken, with his singular mystical sense in shards. The damage, says Diadochus, manifests

---

[55] GC 78.
[56] GC 3.

itself in a multitude of senses pulled in opposing directions as each part of the person claims its own good. The sense of the heart, the sense of the intellect, the corporal senses, the deep sense, the interior senses, need to be pulled back together forming the "total sense of fullness."[57] After baptism or after a conversion experience, when the entire person is penetrated by God's grace and begins to take to the path of reintegration, there yet remains a demonic obstacle to overcome.

Diadochus dedicates much attention to demons; however, he divides them into only two groups: subtle and crass.[58] In other words, we can recognize what kind of a demon is present through its operation. The more subtle demons incite spiritual sin (pride, vainglory, ire), while the crass demons lead us into sins of sensuality. Our author seems to find in Adam and Eve the paradigms of dual demonic influence: when discussing Adam's sin, Diadochus treats it as a disorientation of the natural sense of the soul,[59] while Eve's sin was provoked by immoderation of the corporal senses.[60] Since each of our first parents was enticed by different types of demons, we, their children, all experience the disintegrating effects of both sorts of demons as well as the ensuing weakness from their original Fall.

> [O]n account of the fall through disobedience, this one sense of the soul is distanced from the soul in its movements. Therefore, one part of it is dragged about by the passions, which is why we experience pleasure in the good things of this life; but the other part is often motivated by rational and spiritual delights when we practice moderation, which is why our mind is urged on toward those heavenly beauties when we live according to wisdom. If we learn to persevere in our disdain for worldly goods, we will be able to conjoin the earthly longings of our soul to this disposition of the mind by way of communion with the Holy Spirit who makes this possible for

[57] GC 90.
[58] See GC 81.
[59] See GC 25.
[60] See GC 62.

us. If his divinity does not illumine the treasures of our heart sufficiently, we will not be able to enjoy what is good with an undivided sense, that is, with an integral disposition.[61]

Diadochus describes the nature of spiritual combat as a type of tug-of-war between the Holy Spirit and the devil. So permeated with the sense of spiritual combat is his theology that Diadochus often favors military terminology over vocabulary more proper to the spiritual life. For example, his term *agōnistēs* ("fighter," "wrestler," "athlete," "warrior") and derivatives of that word far outnumber "ascetic" and other terms that indicate a man of God.

Engaging in spiritual combat implies leaving oneself open to be taken advantage of and "dragged about" by the evil one who manipulates our passions. The Holy Spirit, on the other hand, speaks to what is noble and godly in our nature, respectfully attracting us through spiritual delights. These divine advances make known the presence of the Lover and begin to restore lost integrity and communion. This is the beginning of perception of the footprints of the Invisible One. But this perception is only possible through authentic discernment of what the Holy Spirit is accomplishing in the soul. Such discernment permits us to cut through competing interior movements and authentically to desire and encounter that which brings about union and communion, namely the integrating love of God. Such discernment aids us in overcoming divisive tendencies and vices that prevent God's work from coming about in the soul.[62]

Demonic activity manifests itself in several ways, usually by attacking the person in the area of the passions where the individual is weakest: at times the enemy takes advantage of interior states of sorrow such as that caused by God's pedagogical desolation or the sorrow resultant from an immature degree of humility, or the sorrow of this world born of lukewarmness.[63] One of the enemy's more effective weapons is anger (often fruit of the previ-

---

[61] GC 29.
[62] See GC 71, 92.
[63] See GC 85.

ously mentioned states of sorrow). Anger, says Diadochus, is the vice that most darkens the intellective faculties and hinders any sort of union between God and the soul.[64]

Vanity and presumption destroy any likeness to God,[65] while lukewarmness (*akēdia*) leaves the mind and, more particularly, the all-important memory of God (*mnēmē theou*), enchained.[66]

But demons do not limit their activity to inciting the passions of our fallen nature; they toy with our mind, eliciting thoughts, dreams,[67] and, at times, visions.[68]

> Demonic fantasies, on the other hand, are completely the opposite: they do not keep the same image and they do not manifest themselves in a consistent form for long. This they do not willingly do, for in their deceit they only borrow such forms and cannot resist for long. They begin to scream and make lots of threats, often taking the form of soldiers, at times playing on the soul with their shrieks. However, when the mind is purified it recognizes them and even in its dreaming it awakens the body.[69]

Other tactics include engendering false joy, which usually ends in frustration,[70] mitigated concern for demonic activity,[71] and reversal of understanding of good and evil.[72]

Although baptism successfully ousts the demon from the recesses of the soul, the enemy maintains a certain grasp of the interior, which diminishes and becomes an ever more exterior vantage point in proportion to the spiritual progress one makes. As his position of attack alters, the devil is forced to adapt his

---

[64] See GC 26, 62, 71, 87, 96.
[65] See GC 4, 46, 68, 81.
[66] See GC 58, 96.
[67] See GC 38.
[68] See GC 36.
[69] GC 37.
[70] See GC 30.
[71] See GC 33.
[72] See GC 43, 81.

tactics, which can become more subtle. In the case of a warrior who has taken to the path of spiritual combat it is clear that he has no regard for his own evil inclinations. Aware of this, the devil takes to imitating the Holy Spirit,[73] appearing as an angel of light. If the warrior resists, the devil lets loose his arsenal in explosive and open attacks even against the body of the warrior.[74] More subtly still, the devil will attempt to convince the warrior of the strength of his own virtue, above all through the words of those who are already under diabolical influence.[75]

The Role of the Heart

Diadochus's motive in writing to his disciples is "that we come to love God alone with conviction and all the sense of our heart, which is to love God with all our heart, with all our soul and with all our mind. Whoever is moved by God's grace to this is exiled from the world even as he continues to live in the world."[76]

The notion of the heart is yet another key to understanding Diadochan spirituality. Following biblical anthropology, our author makes the heart the epicentre of the human person and the organ of true knowledge.[77] Likewise, those who shun the divine light of knowledge are condemned to live with a "darkened and sterile heart."[78]

The most explicit text on the role of the heart is GC 14.

> One who loves God with the sense of his heart "is known by him" [1 Cor 8:3], because inasmuch as one receives the love of God, according to that measure he will dwell in the love of God. And from that moment onward, he comes to find himself immersed in such an ardent longing for the illumination of

[73] See GC 30.
[74] See GC 81.
[75] See GC 33. In this passage Diadochus is pointing his finger at the Messalians.
[76] GC 40.
[77] See GC 80.
[78] GC 82.

the intellect, penetrating even his bones, that he loses all awareness of himself and he is completely transformed by the love of God. Such a one is present and absent in this life. He has his body for a dwelling place, but vacates it through love. He relentlessly moves toward God in his soul. Once he has transcended his self-love through love for God, his heart becomes consumed in the fire of love and clings to God with unyielding desire. "If we seem out of our senses it was for God; but if we are being reasonable now, it is for your sake" [2 Cor 5:13].

Once the devil has been exorcised from the heart real spiritual life begins. The preceding text offers us the many-faceted role of the heart and reveals its almost universal usage in Diadochan vocabulary. In this passage we see that the heart becomes the receptive vessel of the Holy Spirit, "receiving the love of God." The heart is also the source of longing for intellectual illumination, it includes even that which is mineral in the human person, the bones. The heart is the source of passionate love for God and the organ that God works upon in order for the person to transcend himself in loving ecstasy.

In Diadochus's experiential theology, God's presence makes itself felt in the "sense of the heart." Although for many fathers God could never be felt and for Greek philosophical tradition the heart played no role in the path to God, for Diadochus this is no obstacle. His theology bears within itself a healthy tension between rationality and believing affectivity. Such tension stems not from internal conflict but from the necessary mutual strengthening that shields both reason and affectivity from atrophy. "You will use your lips to confess that Jesus is the Lord and your heart to believe that God has raised him up from the dead" (Rom 10:9). While the importance of the heart does not lead to neglect of a sober measure of reason, Diadochus does not permit the sobriety of his reasonable faith to suffocate the heart, for the heart's task far transcends that of naked reason. "Blessed are the pure of heart, for they shall see God" is the alpha and omega of his epistemology. In other words, grace and the act of faith require the integral person even as they seek to bring about his reintegration.

Beginning with the infusion of baptismal grace, a metamorphosis of the entire person is wrought, encompassing the body and soul along with all his senses and faculties by way of *energeia*. The divine presence active in the human person's every facet forms the glorious body, making precious stones out of the transformed living stones (the bones) for the edifice and making a temple of the Holy Spirit from the heart (the rest of the spiritual person).

Mnēmē Theou *(The Memory of God) and the* Taste of His Goodness

Just as the sanctifying presence of the Holy Spirit poured into the soul ousts the demonic presence, a similar, albeit more extended process of displacement and occupation is played out in the memory and the intellect.

"If one were to think that because we have both good and evil thoughts, both the Holy Spirit and the devil dwell together in the soul,[79] let that one understand that this occurs because we have neither tasted nor seen how good the Lord is."[80] Diadochus clearly wants to avoid a mechanistic vision of grace (and uses the opportunity to take a jab at his nemesis, the Messalians). If purity of heart is efficient in the order of the vision of God, it appears not to be sufficient in light of this text. Purity of heart prepares the occasion for the experience of Christ, yet the experience itself is not self-sufficient purity. Diadochus has a preference for the word "taste" when describing perception of God's presence and the recollection of God's action in one's life. But above all, Diadochus uses "taste" in terms of the result of divine love at work in the soul.[81] Taste bespeaks a certain union and it is precisely this union that will ultimately satisfy the longing for vision and knowledge of God.

---

[79] See GC 78.
[80] GC 85.
[81] See GC 1, 14, 23, 40, 50, 95.

The warrior who has tasted and seen how good the Lord is (see Ps 34:8) has an experience to draw upon amid future spiritual struggles and darkness—all of which are necessary for spiritual progress. Further, such an experience is all-important to the task of reintegration. The apparent incongruity between the physical sense of taste affecting the intellectual sense of sight is proof that the fragments of sense are coming together. This coalescence is proven by the phenomenon of spiritual progress, which embraces the entire person, enlightening the intellect, filling the heart, even as it brings delight to the body.[82]

> If we fervently long for God's virtue, at the outset of our prog-
> ress the Holy Spirit lets the soul taste God's sweetness in all
> the fullness of its sentiment, so that the mind might have keen
> awareness of the ultimate prize for efforts which so please
> God. But later it will often hide the richness of this life-giving
> gift so that, even though we should attain all the other virtues,
> we will consider ourselves as nothing if we do not yet have
> the habit of holy love. . . . From that moment onward, the
> soul suffers much more. On the one hand, it retains the mem-
> ory of spiritual love, yet on the other hand, it cannot attain it
> in the spiritual sense for lack of those trials that bring about
> complete perfection. Therefore it is necessary to abnegate one-
> self in order to arrive at its taste with all one's perception and
> complete certainty. This is so because no one still in the flesh
> can attain his perfection except the saints who make it to
> martyrdom and perfect confession. Therefore, he who has
> attained this is completely transformed and would not
> wantonly grasp for food, for what desire for the goods of this
> world could there be for one who is nourished on divine love?
> Therefore, wisest Paul—that great deposit of knowledge—
> who proclaimed to us the fullness of the future delights of the
> first among the just, says the following: "For the kingdom of
> God is not a matter of food and drink, but of righteousness,
> peace, and joy in the Holy Spirit" [Rom 14:17]. All of that is
> the fruit of perfect charity. And so, those who progress toward

[82] See GC 79.

perfection can continually taste it from here below, but no one can attain perfection, except when the mortal part is swallowed up by life.[83]

The memory of God acts as something of an anchor reaching the depths of the mind where God resides.[84] It makes contemplation possible[85] although it will require persevering effort and vigorous control of memory whose banks also contain relics of what the evil one has committed. For "if his divinity does not illumine the treasures of our heart sufficiently, we will not be able to enjoy what is good with an undivided sense, that is, with an integral disposition."[86]

This "double thought," as Diadochus call it,[87] can be vanquished easily through willed memory of God,[88] "thus rending evil ineffective"[89] and "consuming the dross of evil in the furnace of the memory."[90] When the soul perceives divine action in the depths of the soul, then memory of God progresses from recollection of a past experience of God thus initiating a new and renewing experience. *Mnēmē theou* and experience provide the soul with a virtuous cycle of spiritual progress.

Diadochus is clear in teaching that progress is only possible through spiritual combat. The memory of God brings to mind the taste of God and acts as a sort of efficient commemoration, making present past sacred realities which, in turn, transform one's present. Thus, far beyond a mere activity, the memory of God refers to one's identity, something to which the serious warrior is called "to consecrate himself."[91]

---

[83] GC 90.
[84] See GC 33.
[85] See GC 11.
[86] GC 29.
[87] See GC 88.
[88] See GC 3, 5.
[89] GC 81.
[90] See GC 97.
[91] GC 96.

Why do evil and good coexist in the memory? "It is through the original deceit that [the intellect] once and for all has as a habit the memory of evil."[92] Although Diadochus encourages his disciples to sweep away the memory of evil with a "mere thought," in other passages his presentation is not so facile.

> And so it happens that the soul thinks good and evil things at the same time, just as that man in our example who shivers and feels warm at the same time when he is touched by the warmth of the sun. And so, from the moment in which our mind has slid into this double knowledge, it then produces good and bad thoughts at the same time even though it does not choose to do so—and this above all in those who have come to experience the subtleties of discernment. Even as the mind strives to think of good things, soon it remembers evil things, given that ever since Adam's disobedience human memory is divided in double thought. If we begin then, to fulfill God's commandments with fervent zeal, from that moment onward grace will illumine all of our senses with deep sentiments, as if it were burning our thoughts and penetrating our heart with the peace of unyielding friendship, preparing us to consider things spiritually rather than carnally. This is what frequently occurs to those who approach perfection—to those who ceaselessly keep within their hearts the memory of the Lord Jesus.[93]

Thus, such evil thoughts are made possible thanks to our weakened nature but their genesis is often the evil one. The moral fortitude of the warrior determines whether those evil seeds sprout roots in the heart or not. Should such thoughts be entertained, the body will soon appropriate them and act; hence our Lord's reference to the relationship between evil thoughts and the act of fornication—for "those who are friends of this life's pleasures proceed from thoughts to faults."[94]

---

[92] GC 83.
[93] GC 88.
[94] GC 96. See Mark 7:22-24.

Such persons "do not know that our mind, possessing the subtle faculty of the sense, makes its own the action of the thoughts suggested to it by evil spirits, by way of the flesh as it were. By way of complicity, the body's malleability draws it more toward the soul in a way unknown to us.[95] The flesh always loves to be adulated without measure by such trickery, so it seems that the thoughts sown by demons originate in the heart. On the other hand, we actually do appropriate them when we desire to be gratified by them."[96]

Therefore, "warriors should always keep custody of their thoughts so that the mind can discern the thoughts that pass through it and store in the memory banks those that are good and come from God, while casting out of nature's storage all those that are perverse or diabolical."[97]

In doing so, the memory develops good habits that grow proportionally to the demise of the memory of irrational pleasures and, "walking beyond the half-way point . . . the soul takes to the well-worn path of virtue and joy."[98] Yet the intellect is still in need of reconstructive activity to reintegrate it with the will, the memory, and all the other fragments of original *aisthēsis*. "When we have sealed off every venue through the memory of God, our mind will demand from us an exercise that satisfies its need for activity. Here we must let out a Lord Jesus, as the only perfect way to achieve our goal. No one, it is said, can say 'Jesus is Lord' without the Holy Spirit.[99] So let it [the mind] contemplate this word alone at all times in its interior treasury so as not to return to the imagination. To all who ceaselessly meditate on this holy and glorious Name in the depths of their heart is granted the vision of the light of their minds."[100]

---

[95] See 26:41.
[96] GC 83.
[97] GC 26.
[98] GC 93.
[99] 1 Cor 12:3.
[100] GC 59.

The Jesus Prayer and the Memory of God

When discussing prayer, the majority of Diadochus's comments concern the benefits of prayer. Initially, prayer requires silence,[101] which protects it from passions.[102] Such stillness in prayer makes the mind expansive and this permits a more fruitful discernment of spirits.[103] Prayer is the privileged moment in which the Holy Spirit grants his gifts of knowledge and wisdom.[104] Perseverance in prayer, above all in moments of depression, prepares the soul for subsequent richer gifts of contemplation.[105] On the other hand, inconstancy in prayer will elicit a worldly spirit[106] and stifle the purification process of the soul. Rather, the soul will retain its dross if not ceaselessly submitted to the crucible of divine love through constant contemplation.[107] Other hindrances are anger,[108] sins of excess, or defect in the realm of asceticism.[109]

Since Diadochus is writing to prayer warriors it does not seem fitting to him to present them with a primer on prayer. Given the experiential nature of prayer, Diadochus is in no hurry to present a model experience for everyone to follow; rather, he is content to motivate his readers to continue to advance in their lives dedicated to prayer and offers them rules to discern if their experiences are actually from God or not. Further, in prayer we can speak only like children,[110] and children do not need to be taught how to utter sounds. Thus, he avoids discussing methodology and offers in its stead some basic instructions on the Jesus Prayer.

With his remarks on the memory of God cited above (see GC 83), Diadochus provides us with the key to successful memory of

---

[101] See GC 10.
[102] See GC 62, 68.
[103] See GC 68.
[104] See GC 9.
[105] See GC 73.
[106] See GC 64.
[107] See GC 97.
[108] See GC 26.
[109] See GC 45.
[110] See GC 61.

God: Jesus. Correcting Evagrian intellectualism, which proposes getting beyond the form in prayer—even if that form is the Incarnate Word—Diadochus emphasizes the heart's role, thus opening the door to intimacy with the Person of Christ. As the mind contemplates the sacred Name, the lips recite it, thereby letting the Jesus Prayer begin to integrate mind and body through prayer. But more than provide an aid to original integrity of the sense, the Jesus Prayer is a means toward divine illumination and, ultimately, toward *theosis*. If a purified heart immersed in the memory of God is the prerequisite for the ultimate beatific vision, it is the Jesus Prayer that provides the necessary illumination for this to occur.

Diadochus connects the memory to sense, maintaining that they both have undergone fragmentation as a result of the original Fall. This fragmentation reveals itself in a sort of universal schizophrenia: "And so, from the moment in which our mind has slid into this double knowledge, it then produces good and bad thoughts at the same time even though it does not choose to do so—and this above all in those who have come to experience the subtleties of discernment. Even as the mind strives to think of good things, soon it remembers evil things, given that ever since Adam's disobedience human memory is divided in double thought."[111]

Our author protects the inherent goodness of human nature but explains the universal tendency to evil as part of our passions and the suggestions of the evil one. Yet he leaves our behavior ultimately up to free choice. Once we have developed a habit we begin to define ourselves.[112] The role of free choice is all-important in the reintegration of the divided *nous*, but this reintegration will come about once the memory has been healed and the sense reintegrated.

What follows is a brief exposition on the Diadochan version of the Jesus Prayer and its role in reintegration.

---

[111] GC 88.
[112] See GC 3, 43.

Diadochus is the first witness of the now widespread Jesus Prayer. His version is far simpler than the more common prayer: "Lord Jesus Christ, Son of the living God, have mercy on me, a sinner." Nonetheless, the Diadochan version, "O Lord Jesus,"[113] says much more by merely invoking the Holy Name. It says everything. It surpasses the primordial need we all have of salvation and, in its simplicity, encompasses all reality, for it is God's Name revealed to us, and it is in Jesus Christ that all of salvation history is recapitulated.

To utter "O Lord Jesus" is a turning toward him with trust and longing, an act of faith, hope, and love, and with the certainty of a response. It is the invocation of the Name above all other names (see Phil 2:9-10). While ceaseless memory of God maintains the healthy tension and affection necessary for divine union, the invocation of the Holy Name of Jesus also has a strategic significance. Since it was the devil who provoked the Fall and Christ came to undo his works, it makes sense that invocation of the Holy Name should prove powerful in expelling demonic suggestion: "But if the mind is recollected and perseveres in keeping the fervent memory of the Holy Name of Jesus, it will take strength from that holy and glorious Name using it as a weapon against deception. Thereafter, the impostor leaves off his deceit and throws himself into waging open war against the soul. In this way the mind progresses more in its experience of discernment by recognising the wiles of the evil one."[114]

Nonetheless, invocation of the Holy Name is not a talisman but a way of perpetuating a relationship with Christ. And this relationship requires singularity of heart. To attempt to lead a licentious life and think to invoke fruitfully the Holy Name of Jesus can only lead to frustration: "When the soul is agitated by anger, or blurry-eyed from a hang-over, or discouraged by onerous worries, even if it should forcefully strain itself, the mind cannot attain the memory of the Lord Jesus Christ on its own. Thus darkened by

[113] See GC 59.
[114] GC 31.

its restless passions, the mind becomes a stranger to its own sense. And so the vehemence of the passions entrenches the memory in callousness, the soul's desire finds nowhere to set its seal that the mind might bear the mark of meditation."[115]

Diadochus summarizes his teaching on the Jesus Prayer in the following text:

> When the entire person turns toward the Lord, then [grace], in an ineffable movement, manifests her presence in the heart and awaits once again the soul's movement, permitting that the devil's darts penetrate unperceived unto the most intimate sense, so that in an even more fervent resolve and humble disposition, the soul seeks God. For the rest, if the person begins to advance in the observance of the commandments and continuously invokes the Lord, then the fire of holy grace spreads even to the external senses of his heart, burning the chaff of the human soil completely. Thus, even the demonic darts land far from these parts and only lightly pierce the passionate part of the soul. Finally, when the combatant has dressed himself in all the virtues and, above all, perfect poverty, then grace illumines all of his nature with an ever deeper sentiment, setting it ablaze with great love for God. From that moment onward, the demonic bowshots are extinguished outside of the body's senses. Thus the breeze of the Holy Spirit which moves the heart toward those winds of peace extinguishes even those demon-borne fiery darts in midair.[116]

Here the role of the Jesus Prayer and its part in the reintegration of the sense is laid out: Fidelity to God's commandments makes the invocation of the Holy Name fruitful. The Name brings about the memory of God, which, in turn, prepares the path to union with God. Diadochus often mentions obedience to God's commandments and the invocation of Jesus/*mnēmē theou* in relation to each other. To attempt such obedience or recollection is only

---

[115] GC 61.
[116] GC 85.

possible for those under the Holy Spirit's influence,[117] for it is a realization of the second baptismal gift. Baptismal grace bestows two gifts on the soul: a renewal of one's status as image of God and the opportunity to restore the divine likeness. In bestowing the second gift, infinitely surpassing the first, the Holy Spirit "hopes to bring about [this transformation] with our coopera-tion."[118] On the level of *bios* this requires obedience to God and ascetical practices, while on the level of *nous* it demands the con-stant memory of the Lord. This complementary operation spreads to all the senses and unites them in a common purpose. The ex-penditure is far outweighed by its benefits. Not only is eternal salvation promised in the next life, a sort of psychological healing is wrought in this life, thanks to the effects of asceticism, prayer, and the effects of the reintegration of the senses and its resultant joy.

> So let it [the *nous*] contemplate this word alone at all times in its interior treasury so as not to return to the imagination. To all who ceaselessly meditate on this holy and glorious Name in the depths of their heart can see at last the light of their minds. Thus tamed by such an exacting effort of thought, every stain on the soul's surface is consumed in ardent feeling, for it is said, our God is a consuming fire [Deut 4:24]. Therefore the Lord invites the soul to immense love of his own glory, for persevering in the mind's memory of that glorious and most desirable Name with an ardent heart, which produces in us a habitual love of his goodness which, from that moment on-ward, nothing can hinder. This is the precious pearl [see Matt 13:36] which is obtained upon having dispossessed oneself of all one's belongings and whose discovery brings about in-effable joy.[119]

Continual prayer is rooted in love. It is the result of having sold everything to obtain Christ, the precious pearl. Freed up from

[117] See GC 16.
[118] GC 89.
[119] GC 59.

egoism and passions the warrior begins to discover Christ in his fullness and, as a result, himself in his original beauty.[120] Proper to a person who is friendly with virtue is to consume all that is earthly in his heart through the memory of God, so that, little by little, evil is consumed by the fire of the recollection of goodness, and the soul returns perfectly to its natural shine but with an even greater splendor.[121]

Contemplation has a direct role in the order of eschatological *theosis* and is, therefore, an exercise in the theological virtue of hope. Hope, holds Diadochus, is "an emigration of the intellect in love, moving toward those things that await us."[122] Emigration is the language of ecstasy, privileged knowledge gained only from direct experience of God. Indeed for Diadochus, "Knowledge [is] unawareness of oneself in the ecstasy of God."[123] He returns to this ecstatic paradigm stating that in contemplation a person "loses all awareness of himself and is completely transformed by the love of God. Such a one is present and absent in this life. He has his body for a dwelling place, but vacates it through love. He relentlessly moving toward God in his soul. Once he has transcended his self-love through love for God, his heart becomes consumed in the fire of love and clings to God with unyielding desire."[124]

Although all contemplation is guided by the theological virtues,[125] it is dangerous to attempt contemplation unless one has attained a certain degree of enlightenment.[126] Rather than postulate spiritual elitism, Diadochus, as always, has the spiritual well-being of his disciples at heart. Since all "knowledge consists wholly of love,"[127] to attempt contemplation without having at-

---

[120] See GC 59.
[121] GC 97.
[122] GC Def. 2.
[123] GC Def. 5.
[124] GC 14.
[125] See GC 1.
[126] See GC 8.
[127] GC 92.

tained an adequate degree of love and dedication would be presumptuous and could only end in disaster. For Diadochus, prayer and asceticism are exteriorizations of an existent relationship, and to purport a quality of relationship with God that does not yet exist could only spell one's undoing. Hence it is humility that most helps one attain a healthy selflessness, forgetting one's own success and progress[128] in order to pray as one ought according to one's state. But once a person has gotten beyond the sensibly fervent prayer of the beginner and arrived at the prayer "beyond all expansion"[129] then he should seek this state without ceasing, spending the "greatest amount of time in it."[130] For it is only contemplation that can fill the heart with burning desire for God[131] to then begin following in the footprints of the Invisible One.[132]

Fear, Penthos, *Tears, and* Apatheia

Considering the alternatives—eternal glory and its requisite long, arduous purification, or the prospect of eternal loss—a degree of fear seems reasonable. Scripture's presentation of judgment and eternal condemnation certainly provokes a salutary fear. Nonetheless, what is one to make of that reality supported by the scriptural declaration that the fear of the Lord is the beginning of wisdom (Ps 111:10) balanced against Christ's frequent counsel, "Have no fear" (Matt 28:10)?

Fear is the passion that responds to a present or imminent danger. There are particular modes of fear. In relationship to God (psychological ills such as scruples aside), the mode of fear experienced depends on the spiritual state of the individual. Diadochus treats each mode of fear as symptomatic of one's spiritual health, a sort of indicator of where one is on the path of reintegration.

---

[128] See GC Def. 6.
[129] See GC 68, 73.
[130] GC 68.
[131] See GC 7.
[132] See GC 69.

Initial fear of God, the fear of punishment proper to novices in the spiritual life, is accompanied by newly found contrition (*penthos*), an attitude, unlike fear, that dare not change so long as one is in this world. This attitude propels the disciple of Christ to seek out penance, to make reparation, to weep for the offended God, and to give oneself over to the love of God.[133] Growing in love for God balances out fear until such moment when true love finally casts out all fear (see 1 John 4:18).

Beginning with the fourth century the phenomenon of the gift of tears has been appropriated by ascetic language. This is a common feature in Byzantine spirituality and is frequently found in Western spirituality as well. The Greek fathers hold tears in esteem, as proof of authentic conversion and pure love for God. "Blessed are those who mourn" (Matt 5:4) applies to the follower of Christ who, having sought consolation and glory in this world, repents. Thus, rather than a pessimistic presentation of Christian spirituality, this teaching reflects the guaranteed path to beatitude. Tears purify the heart of the penitent as much as they reveal conversion. They are a sign of gratitude for God's favor, for a tear-washed face reveals a purified soul. Tears, in effect, are a grace.

According to the Greek fathers, a fruit of the work of grace in the soul is *apatheia*—the mind's freedom and independence from carnal *pathos*—passion. This implies an interior strength born of asceticism and blossoming into ardent love for God. With this in mind, it should be clear that *apatheia* is by no means an end in itself but rather it opens the door to true knowledge (*gnōsis*) of the love of God. To underline the introductory role of *apatheia*, Diadochus opens his most important work by defining "faith [as] an impassible [*apathēs*] consideration of God."[134] Such interior self-dominion and quiet permit grace to work fruitfully and also engender better self-knowledge—both necessary for the all-important task of discernment of spirits.

---

[133] See Mark the Hermit's *De Paenitentiae*, 11, PG 65:981A.
[134] GC Def. 1.

Discernment of Spirits

After the work of grace and its effects we come to the other pole of Diadochus's spirituality.

A considerable portion of the path toward reintegration is covered through sound discernment of spirits. With true discernment the disciple penetrates the mysteries of God even as he uncovers the secrets of the human heart. It requires a spiritual perspicuity that sees past flesh, space, and time. Discernment therefore involves the art of identifying the true causes of interior movements: divine, diabolical, or human. Such movements include consolations, desolations, images, and dreams, and part of the task of their discernment is knowledge of self: of one's tendencies and aspirations, present state of soul, psychological state, and so forth.

For Diadochus, discernment of spirits is where theology and *praxis* meet. It requires learning to refine the "taste" of God's presence and discovering that true theology is not information about God but an experience of him. Therefore, real discernment has to be done in prayer; otherwise the warrior loses the taste for God and his relationship grows cold. Prayer without discernment has its own dangers, as it exposes the warrior to the deceits of the enemy. Learning infallibly to discern the "footprints of the Invisible One"[135] means that one has reached the heights of the spiritual life as a "theologian."

A true theologian has experienced God in an ineffable way, and such divine encounters become the standard by which to judge; otherwise, "we will not gladly forego present delights if we do not yet fully taste the sweetness of God with all our sense."[136] The encounter with the living God presents the warrior with a wholly new parameter. It is precisely this otherness of the source of these new experiences that can perplex the neophyte as well as the experienced follower of Christ. Therefore, Diadochus intends to help the reader discover the source of the interior movements

---

[135] See GC 1, 69.
[136] GC 44.

of consolations and desolations, dreams and visions, that make up the spiritual life.

Diadochus calls consolation a "movement"[137] that consists of divine love that inflames and impels the soul, seeking its reintegration so that "every part of the soul is ineffably united to the sweetness of this divine desire in an attitude of unending simplicity."[138] Symptoms of divine consolation include:

- Consolations without previous cause, mediation, or "imagination."[139]

- Certainty that the motion comes from the Holy Spirit.[140]

- Profound peace to the soul.[141]

- A fire within the heart and soul.[142]

The enemy, too, can use consolation to deceive the warrior. Diadochus mentions that this often happens at certain times of the day or during certain activities. "Satan begins sweetly to lull during the night's rest, when one is just starting to fall into a light sleep."[143]

Already differences are manifest. As opposed to the deep peace of the Holy Spirit, the evil spirit produces "sweetness," not nearly as deep or long-lasting as God's gift. Other symptoms of diabolical consolation include:

- Interior sweetness is briefly accompanied by inappropriate thoughts.[144]

- It is disordered and brings about disorder if followed.[145]

---

[137] GC 33.
[138] GC 34.
[139] See GC 33.
[140] See GC 33.
[141] See GC 35.
[142] See GC 33, 34.
[143] GC 31.
[144] See GC 33.
[145] See GC 32.

- It produces interior agitation.[146]

- It seeks to make the warrior stumble on his path toward re-integration, bringing about interior division through vain consolation. In order to accomplish this the evil one will try to hide his presence in an attempt to convince the warrior that God is at work.[147] If he succeeds in this, he can be assured of sowing confusion in the heart and mind of the unwary warrior.

As mentioned before, the memory of God and, in particular, the Jesus Prayer are the weapons of choice for such encounters. This prayer has a threefold effect: it works as a defense against evil spirits, it engenders union with Christ, and it acts as a litmus test in the discernment of spirits.

Perhaps more subtle a subject to discern is that of the genesis of desolation. Diadochus discusses two reasons for desolation when the source is God. In the first case, God's motives are peda-gogical or corrective, producing spiritual dryness and darkness in the soul of the warrior, hiding his presence deep in the recesses of the soul.[148] Through such a maneuvre God provokes the devil to attack the warrior with the intention that he experience the enemy's assaults and, in turn, learn to seek divine assistance. "Indeed, corrective desolation does not deprive the soul of divine light in any way whatsoever. As I have already said, frequently grace merely hides its presence within the soul, so that impelled by the devil's bitterness, the soul progresses though seeking God's assistance with all fear and great humility, thus recognizing little by little the evil deeds of the enemy."[149]

For the soul advancing along the path of spiritual progress, the greatest enemy is spiritual pride. Pedagogical desolation intends to check the surge of pride and bring the warrior to new levels of

---

[146] See GC 35.
[147] See GC 33.
[148] See GC 85.
[149] GC 86.

humility. "God's pedagogical desolation brings about in the soul profound sorrow, humiliation, and a degree of despair, so that the glory-seeking and timorous parts be led to humility, as is fitting. Quickly it brings fear of God and tears of confession upon the heart and a deep desire for beautiful silence."[150]

God also disposes of desolation as a means to punish the soul that has wandered from the true path. "That desolation which occurs on account of infidelity to God leaves the soul filled with despair mixed with faithlessness, pride, and anger."[151] This is the logical consequence of one's own choices. In fact, it would be a contradiction for God to reward the soul with consolation if it had made evil choices or decided to live in mediocrity. God's mercy lets the soul experience the fruit of its choices with a view to its turning back to him.

Both desolations work toward spiritual good in one who knows how to respond in such a spiritual state. Chapter 87 offers the rules of discernment for such cases: "Understanding the experience of both types of desolation we must then go to God with the dispositions proper to each."

> [1.] In the first case we ought to offer Him thanksgiving along with contrition as the one disciplining our undisciplined mind in the school of consolation, and for having taught us as a good father the difference between virtue and vice.
>
> [2.] In the second case we should offer Him unceasing confession of our sins, tears without end, and greater solitude, so that by way of added effort we can petition God to look upon our heart as he did before. But one ought to know that when the battle between Satan and the soul takes the form of a confrontation—here I am referring to the purgative desolation—grace, as I said before, hides itself but operates invisibly aiding the soul in order to show its enemies that victory belongs to the soul alone.[152]

---

[150] GC 87.
[151] GC 87.
[152] GC 87.

Another phenomenon that requires discernment of spirits is that of dreams and visions. Chapters 36–40 are dedicated to this teaching. Diadochus is categorically opposed to visions, not because God is incapable of manifesting himself through such a means but rather because they would contradict God's desire for us to walk in the twilight of faith.[153] His suspicion of visions leads him to instruct his disciples to reject any such image that appears to them as "patent deception of the enemy."[154]

Dreams, on the other hand, are not always diabolical at their source. "Dreams that reveal to the soul the love of God are sure indicators of a healthy soul. . . . [T]hey approach the soul completely reasonably, heaping upon it spiritual delight. Therefore, even after the body has awakened, the soul seeks the joy of the dream with great desire."[155]

Quite another thing are those dreams which come from the enemy.

> Demonic fantasies, on the other hand, are completely the opposite: they do not keep the same image and they do not manifest themselves in a consistent form for long. This they do not willingly do, for in their deceit they only borrow such forms and cannot resist for long. They begin to scream and make lots of threats, often taking the form of soldiers at times playing on the soul with their shrieks. However, when the mind is purified it recognizes them and even in its dreaming it awakens the body. Other times it delights at having discovered the deceit. Therefore, confuting them over and over again in the same dream, it sparks his fury.[156]

These are opposed to the divinely inspired dreams that do not "go from one image to another, nor do they frighten the senses, nor do they sneer or suddenly show a sombre expression."[157]

[153] See GC 36.
[154] GC 36.
[155] GC 37.
[156] GC 37.
[157] GC 37.

Further, "dreams are almost always nothing more than vague thoughts or the forms of errant thoughts."[158] In other words, most often there is no supernatural source for the dreams made of one's own jumbled thoughts and recollections.

In spite of his recognition of divinely induced dreams, Diadochus seems suspicious of all of them and thinks it virtuous to remain skeptical, regardless of the experience.[159] Entrusting oneself to dreams proves too great a danger and provides a shaky foundation for decision making. For "even if God's goodness should send down a vision to us and yet we were never to accept it, our much longed for Lord Jesus Christ would not be angry with us on that account, because he knows we come to this on account of diabolical deceptions."[160]

Thus far we have seen that for Diadochus discernment is another word for cooperation with grace. By way of discernment, which offers "light of true knowledge," we progress along the path toward divine light. Discernment entails following the footprints of the Invisible One by way of the intellectual sense, which means developing a taste for the things of God, an experience that leaves us loving him with still more conviction and decision. In other words, rather than a mere a source of knowledge, discernment of spirits offers light in order to act.

Our author insists that such light and action are only possible if the disciple is willing to engage in spiritual combat, since that is necessary for spiritual growth and maturity. True discernment amid trials and darkness, generously engaging in spiritual combat, all contribute to the purification of the whole person and the soul's reintegration. Yet, this is a fight in flux. The tactics of the enemy and the action of the Holy Spirit are, to a certain extent, determined by the spiritual state of the individual. The following text makes it clear that Diadochus recognizes rules and modes of discernment proper to each stage of the spiritual life:

---

[158] GC 38.
[159] GC 38.
[160] GC 38.

One thing is the joy of the beginner; quite another is that of the perfect. One is not free from a wandering mind, while the other enjoys the strength of humility. And between the two are found godly sorrow and painless tears, for truly, *in much wisdom there is much knowledge and he who has increase of knowledge has increase of sorrow* [Sir 1:18].[161]

The Stages of the Spiritual Life

The brief analysis of the Jesus Prayer began by highlighting the relationship between obedience, memory, the reintegration of the sense, and the healing of the *nous*. Each of these elements is a microcosm of Diadochus's entire spiritual itinerary. What follows is a presentation of Diadochus's description of the stages of the spiritual life as well as the counsels he prescribes to achieve such progress under the guise of discernment of spirits.

A word about the nature of the stages of spiritual progress is in order. Although this teaching has a biblical foundation, and the support of the patristic, scholastic, and Spanish mystical traditions, it often suffers from misrepresentation by those spiritual directors who seem to fear that knowledge of this teaching might engender spiritual pride or simply confuse the faithful, and who therefore shun it. Note that these spiritual directors do not deny the truth of the teaching, but are simply hesitant to teach it. On the other hand, treatment of this subject has been rather hackneyed since the seventeenth century as writers have attempted to reproduce this sublime teaching in their manuals, neatly divided into ascetical and mystical theology. Such books have managed to categorize the stages and their corresponding symptoms in a way foreign to the mystical tradition and have forfeited what is simple and profound. Beyond those deficiencies, the two areas that have most suffered have been the role of the gifts of the

---

[161] GC 60.

Holy Spirit and the unity of the one divine project in the life of the Christian, played out through the successive stages.[162] Evidence of the phenomenon of spiritual growth and the need to strive for progress can be found in the words of our Lord who indicates progressive stages from servant to friend (see John 15:15) and from friend to sons in the Son (see Matt 28:10; John 21:5). Paul, although he classifies people as carnal or spiritual (see Rom 7:14), favors the analogy of physical growth from infants to mature (see 1 Cor 3:1-3; Eph 4:12-16) to describe the stages of the spiritual life. As if to prove that all analogies are imperfect, Paul emphasizes the role of personal striving in the order of perfection and completion in Christ (see Phil 3:12-15) as opposed to normal, unwilled physical transformation. Hebrews 5:12-14 also reflects Paul's analogy of spiritual infants who need to mature.

Greek philosophy had already come up with its own division of people classified as *praktikoi* (those dedicated to the active life) and *theoretikoi* (those dedicated to the contemplative life). The Greek fathers adopted this usage, applying the *praktikos* term to those still in the stage of active purification and reserving the term *theoretikos* for those who had achieved mystical knowledge of God. This was the case with Origen and the Alexandrian School. This distinction was further developed by the Cappadocians from whom Evagrius inherited part of his teaching.

Evagrius holds that the first stage, *praktikos*, consists of the acquisition of virtues that ends in dispassion (*apatheia*). Such an achievement permits the dedicated person to advance to the stage of *gnōsis*, which bears within itself two levels: contemplation of material beings and contemplation of immaterial beings known through conformity to divine reason, the Logos, the Source of all visible and invisible. This leads to the contemplation of God, *theologia*, the supreme knowledge and the ultimate stage of the spiritual life.

---

[162] Examples of this are Giovanni Battista Scaramelli, *Direttorio Ascetico* and his *Direttorio Mistico* (1751), and Tomasso di Valgornera, *Mystica theologia divi Thomae* (1662).

Diadochus mirrors his contemporary, Mark the Hermit,[163] in identifying the stages with the following terms:

1. "Beginners" (*archomenoi*), "infants" (*nepiazontes*), "novices" (*eisagogikoi*), or "those being purified" (*katharizomenoi*).
2. "Middle stage" (*mesoi*) or "those who have been purified" (*katharisthēntes*).
3. "Perfect" (*teleioi*).

Diadochus is careful not to so isolate the signs of each stage as if they had nothing to do with the life of the soul at other moments of the spiritual journey. Nonetheless, he is keen to identify the signs (and their idiosyncrasies) most common to each stage and the corresponding action to be taken in discerning them and addressing them. Further, the path toward reintegration has specific patterns proper to each stage, determined by the predominant aspect of the spiritual life undergoing purification at that moment. Although the Holy Spirit focuses his purifying action on a certain aspect of the interior, the other elements of the soul are not ignored. Rather, they are obliquely affected. For example, to take the path of reintegration requires a fundamental option proper to a first conversion. But such a decision is not sufficient to stay the course. The decision must be renewed frequently along the path to spiritual perfection.

Once the *choice* has been made the predominant aspect of the first stage is shown to be the purification of the *memory*. Having passed to the middle stage, the soul undergoes a purification of the *sense*. The perfect, in turn, experience the crucible of the purified *intellect*. Nonetheless, each stage contains some element of the others. It is interesting to note that, like the prodigal son who had to retrace each wayward step in order to be restored to his former dignity, beginning with the most recent step, so too does Diadochus's path of reintegration entail a reverse route of

---

[163] See *De Pean.*, 7; PG 65:976C; 11; PG 65:981B. This terminology is adopted by John Climacus, as well.

disintegration: obfuscation of the intellect, fragmentation of the sense, failing of the memory of God, and ultimately the choice for evil.[164]

As the soul journeys toward reintegration, progress manifests itself not only in the new spiritual situations and phenomena but above all in the transformation of those elements that will accompany the person throughout his itinerary. Paying close attention to the effect of grace and its manifestations in the four areas mentioned above (choice, memory, sense, intellect) as well as to the corresponding states of love—and its balance with fear, tears, prayer, virtue, the nature of trials, discernment of spirits, and the dangers proper to each stage—we begin to see with more clarity—the genius and the completeness of Diadochus's theology.

The First Stage—Beginners

"If we fervently long for God's virtue, at the outset of our progress the Holy Spirit lets the soul taste God's sweetness in all the fullness of its sentiment, so that the mind might have keen awareness of the ultimate prize for efforts which so please God."[165] The Holy Spirit rewards the godly choice for following Christ with consolation, although this joy cannot compare with the joy of the perfect.[166] For such initial joy can be only partial, as "when someone in the winter season who stands out in the open facing East at the break of day, the front of his body is warmed by the sun, but his back is deprived of all warmth because the sun is not yet over his head. That is how it is for those who are just beginning spiritual activity."[167]

But such initial joy, a logical consequence of the newly formed relationship with God, also acts as a preparation for trials that are sure to come. One trial proper to this stage results from the neophyte's spiritual, and perhaps psychological, instability, teetering

---

[164] See GC 29.
[165] GC 90.
[166] See GC 60.
[167] GC 88.

between euphoric, presumptuous consolation and depressive desolation.[168] Further,

> the word of knowledge teaches us that the novice soul given over to theology is easily disturbed by a host of passions, above all ire and hatred. She suffers this more on account of her own personal spiritual progress than on account of a great number of demons stirring up the passions. Thus, so long as the soul is inclined toward worldly mindedness, she will even stand idly by, unaffectedly watching justice trampled underfoot by someone because she is more concerned with her own cares and such a soul does not look to God.[169]

The nature of the choice for God proper to this stage of spiritual progress takes the form of obedience, the virtue that ultimately opens the door to divine love.[170] This is a virtue Christ loved "passionately," in proportion to his love for the Father who commanded him.[171] Further, love for obedience engenders humility,[172] which is the "true seal of piety."[173] It permits the warrior to forget about self and one's achievements[174] and importance,[175] to become little, and to allow God to treat oneself as a mother would her child.[176]

Humility is a particularly difficult virtue to acquire[177] since it is heaped upon the warrior through physical ailments, the scorn of others, or one's own interior mental trials, convincing him that he is worse than the rest.[178] Nonetheless, it is precisely the ongoing choice for humility that permits the subsequent transformation

---

[168] See GC 69.
[169] GC 71.
[170] See GC 41.
[171] See GC 41.
[172] See Vision 7; GC 41.
[173] Sermon 2.
[174] See GC Def. 6.
[175] See GC 13.
[176] See GC 65.
[177] See GC 95.
[178] See GC 95.

to commence. "When the passions are stirred, silent battle must ensue using prayer and charity—all done in humility."[179]

The first stage of the spiritual journey sees tears stemming from fear of the evil one,[180] proof of imperfect love. Tears of contrition[181] also appear in the eyes of the newly converted, with their sins still fresh in their unpurified memories.

In this first stage, the memory acts as an instrument for discerning spirits as well as purification, above all when invoking the Holy Name of Jesus. Memory can turn one's attention away from evil[182] even as it fortifies the warrior. Important for this stage is how the memory of the Holy Name acts as a sort of exorcising rite, forcing the evil one to reveal himself even when he has succeeded in deceiving the warrior through false consolation.[183] Exercise of the memory of God engenders, in turn, true consolation, which

> is brought about when the body is fully awake or even when it begins to feel sleep coming on, when one has bonded oneself to [God's] love through the fervent memory of his Name. False consolation, on the other hand, is, as I have said, always produced when the warrior enters into light sleep, half forgetful of God. Thus, the first type comes from God who manifestly exhorts the souls of the warriors to a great outpouring of reverential love. Whereas, the other type accustomed to influencing the soul with winds of deceit, attempts to rob the healthy mind of its experience of the memory of God while the body sleeps. But if the mind maintains the attentive memory of the Lord Jesus, as I mentioned, the enemy's apparently pleasant and mild breeze dissipates, and it then joyfully leaps into battle with its second weapon after grace: the confidence that comes from experience.[184]

---

[179] GC 96.
[180] See GC 86.
[181] See GC 87.
[182] See GC 3, 56, 81.
[183] See GC 31.
[184] GC 32.

The exercise of the memory of God, Christocentric to be sure, restores the soul to its original beauty with greater glory.[185] It frees the *nous* of the fantasies that inhibit true prayer[186] and affords the warrior a glimpse of the light of his own intellect in the depths of the heart.[187] The memory of Jesus arouses true love for goodness, thus replacing the memory of accrued disordered attachments of the previous life.[188] And since the memory of the Lord Jesus must become unceasing, it constitutes the type of prayer proper to this stage.[189] Such prayer must be independent of place since it consists of an attitude of prayer and a longing of the heart rather than something voiced.[190]

The exercise of the memory of God is not merely something to do. Invoking that memory acts as a bridge, linking the warrior to his future glory and anchoring him in his preternatural past. Originally, human nature included one sense that had God for its object. The task of reintegration will require the novice to work from the exterior inward. This work will include fasting and moderation in drink.[191] The self-control common to all virtues must not limit itself to the cultivation of bodily virtues but reach into the very interior, purifying the soul.[192] The life of asceticism and fidelity to Christ, in a word, the choice for Christ, demands totality. Although as far as Diadochus is concerned the age of martyrs is past, true Christians are not excluded from this honor. In a time of peace for the church, the bodies and souls of warriors must still undergo purification and trial—those opportunities sought actively and those passively received. Fidelity to grace in such moments constitutes "the second martyrdom."[193]

---

[185] See GC 97.
[186] See GC 68.
[187] See GC 59.
[188] See GC 32, 59, 88.
[189] See GC 56, 97.
[190] See GC 97.
[191] See GC 47, 52.
[192] See GC 42.
[193] GC 94.

From the moment of baptism, as I mentioned, grace hides itself in the depths of the mind, its presence concealed even from our very senses. But when one begins to long for God with total conviction, then in sublime colloquy it communicates a portion of its wealth to the soul through the intellect's senses. From the moment in which he has firmly set his heart upon complete possession of what he has discovered his desire is such that he is happily willing to abandon all of this world's present goods in order truly to acquire the field in which the treasure of this life lies hidden.[194]

Although the *nous* dominates the third stage, it already experiences the beginnings of grace's transformation, albeit not without human cooperation. The infusion of grace warms the heart with ineffable movements,[195] awakening the mind to hidden realities and pointing it toward the possession of God.

The novice warrior experiences grace as enlightening and encouraging; it urges him to follow the footprints of the Invisible One.[196] "At the outset of our progress, the Holy Spirit lets the soul taste God's sweetness in a total sense of fullness, so that the mind might have keen awareness of the ultimate prize for efforts which so please God."[197] Nonetheless, as a beginner, prayer still suffers from images and fantasies that hinder perfect union.[198] Further, the untamed passions and the failure to have acquired perfect *apatheia* weighs down the warrior in this struggle.

In spite of the spiritual consolations experienced at the beginning, suffering is not wanting thanks to the still disintegrated personality. Discernment of spirits is more fundamental at this stage, distinguishing between good and evil. But all of this is carried out amid one's own thoughts, affections, attractions, and sentiments, which are not necessarily always pure. In other words, it is not enough correctly to discern what is good and evil, unless

---

[194] GC 77.
[195] See GC 85.
[196] See GC 69.
[197] GC 90.
[198] See GC 73.

one humbly and adequately has taken stock of all that is occurring in the soul. Therefore, "warriors always should keep custody of their thoughts so that the mind can discern the thoughts that pass through it and store in the memory banks those that are good and come from God, while casting out of nature's storage all those that are perverse or diabolical."[199]

Further, although the Holy Spirit bestows a certain perception of grace on the neophyte and "at first it is normal for grace to illumine the soul with its own light with great perception,"[200] such ones "have their hearts only partially warmed by holy grace. Thus their mind can begin its fruitful spiritual thought, but the visible parts of the heart continue thinking according to the flesh, since not all their members are illumined in the depth of their perception by the light of holy grace."[201]

Following the normal pattern of spiritual progress after the first conversion, the warrior discovers that his battle with sin takes place interiorly—in the area of thoughts and unfortunate words, unlike his old life, which exteriorized sin through action. "Therefore it is necessary that they consecrate themselves to the observance of the holy commandments and a profound memory of the Lord of glory. For *he who keeps the commandment knows no evil word*,[202] which means he will not be distracted by evil thoughts and words."[203]

At this stage, "when the soul enjoys the fullness of its innate fruits, it sings the psalms with more strength and prefers to pray with a louder voice. . . . The former disposition is accompanied by joy, thus awakening the imagination. . . . In this way the seeds of contemplation sown in tears are made manifest in the soil of the heart because of the joyful hope of its harvest."[204]

[199] GC 26.
[200] GC 69.
[201] GC 88.
[202] Eccl 8:5.
[203] GC 96.
[204] GC 73.

The Second Stage—Mesoi

The two predominant elements in the second stage are *aisthēsis* and *apatheia*. More precisely, the hallmark of *apatheia* indicates that the warrior has made the necessary progress in the first stage to develop the habit of generosity and virtue when confronted with temptation. For "impassibility [*apatheia*] does not consist in not being attacked by demons, because then we would all have to depart from this world, as the Apostle says [see 1 Cor 5:10], but in remaining undefeated when we are attacked by them."[205] Further, having advanced considerably, and obtained a proportionate degree of *apatheia*, the soul becomes more receptive to the action of the Holy Spirit[206] and is more awake to his movements in the partially restored sense.[207]

Diadochus cites as another sign that the warrior is approaching the firm acquisition of *apatheia* that he is capable of accepting the cross of illness and suffering with virtue.[208] Such an attitude will be necessary for the warrior in this stage, so fraught with purifying vicissitudes.

> This is when the devil of hatred increases his attacks on the souls of the warriors in such a way that they accuse of hatred even those who love them, and their kiss conceals mortal hatred. From that moment onward, the soul suffers much more. On the one hand, it retains the memory of spiritual love, yet on the other hand, it cannot attain it in the spiritual sense for lack of those trials that bring about complete perfection. Therefore, it is necessary to abnegate oneself in order to arrive at its taste with all one's sense and complete certainty. . . .[209]
> As a result, grace, by way of the spiritual sense, makes the body rejoice with ineffable exultation in those who advance in knowledge.[210]

---

[205] GC 98.
[206] See GC 25.
[207] See GC 71.
[208] See GC 54.
[209] GC 90.
[210] GC 79.

The increased reintegration affords a newfound simplicity in the soul, producing an ever more wordless prayer. With ease, the soul encounters God "in the solitude of her own heart with joy and listlessness."[211] Diadochus uses several terms to describe the experience of God, the consuming Fire, with recourse to synonyms of warmth, fire, and heat. This interior fire brings assurance of God's presence but also enlightens the intellect, revealing ever more clearly the nature of one's past and present state of soul, thus effecting a heightened sorrow for one's own offenses. Knowledge of one's own fault as well as the awareness that one has given scandal—even to worldly people—is yet another cause of great mortification.[212]

Further, "the Lord permits the soul to be burdened by demons in order to teach her the value of discernment of good and evil, and to render her humbler still, because the discomfiting diabolical thoughts shame the soul even as it is purified."[213]

Such experiences heighten the warrior's ability to discriminate. The perceptive faculty (*aisthēsis*) of the intellect is made up of this ability to discern the tastes of different experiences. After attaining a certain degree of *apatheia*, the warrior becomes aware of the vastness of God's rich grace and can prefer nothing else in its place. *Aisthēsis*, the experiential knowledge of God, is reintegrated by the action of the Holy Spirit in the purified soul. Thus equipped he can properly taste God (note Diadochus's use of *geusthai* and *geusis* ["taste"], *hēdutēs* ["sweet taste"] and *glukutēs* ["sweetness"]). The memory of such experiences is stored in the purified mind and serves as a reserve in times of trial. "The sense of the mind has a precise taste for the things it discerns. Just as our corporal sense of taste flawlessly distinguishes between good and bad tastes when we are healthy and we are therefore drawn to good things, so too, when our mind starts to move about freely and without much worry, it is capable of feeling the wealth of divine

---

[211] GC 73.
[212] See GC 92.
[213] GC 77.

consolation without ever being dragged here and there by any-thing that could oppose it."[214]

Upon seeing the warrior's conviction and the work of the Holy Spirit advance in the area of the sense, the enemy flies into a rage in an attempt to hinder this work and "violently takes the soul prisoner by way of the bodily senses, especially when they find us negligent in running the race of piety, inciting it—murderers that they are—to do what it does not want to do."[215] Thus, for "those who are in the middle stage of combat,"[216] the enemy piques the increased awareness of one's own physical weakness, injustices from others, and one's own interior struggles in the area of thoughts; they are driven to new levels of humility.[217]

The experience of joy is followed by periods of "spiritual tears followed by a longing for silence. For the memory keeps its warmth when the voice is moderated and it prepares the heart to express itself with tearful and joyous thoughts."[218] Whereas the tears of the first stage were a product of contrition, the quality of tears in this second stage are, above all, tears of gratitude[219] shed painlessly amid "godly sorrow."[220]

Diadochus compares the increased presence and influence of the Holy Spirit to oil thrown upon raging seas, bringing calm, lulling the soul to rest. Indeed, if one "perseveres in it . . . it is continuously assuaged by the fear of God. . . . Fear of the Lord Jesus brings about a certain purification in his warriors, since the fear of the Lord is pure, enduring forever [Ps 19:10]."[221] The in-crease of love mitigates the balance of fear in this stage as fear gives way to love—albeit, an imperfect love.[222]

---

[214] GC 30.
[215] GC 79.
[216] GC 95.
[217] GC 95.
[218] GC 73.
[219] See GC 27.
[220] GC 60.
[221] GC 35.
[222] GC 16.

Progress brings with it its own subtleties. Discernment of spirits is no longer a crass decision between good and evil, but a testing field for the spiritual maturity of the warrior (see 1 Cor 14:12). Spiritual decision making entails choosing between good and better. Diadochus leaves us the following example:

> As the body tastes earthly sweetness and has a sure sense for it, so too the mind can infallibly recognize the Holy Spirit's consolation far above those of the flesh: Taste, it is said, and see that the Lord is good [Ps 133:9]. Through the exercise of love, the mind retains the memory of this taste, infallibly discerning the best things and choosing them, as the Saint says: my prayer is that your love for each other may increase more and more and never stop improving your knowledge and deepening your sense, so that you can always recognize what is best [Phil 1:9-10].[223]

Diadochus compares the mode of discernment at this stage to the craft of fishermen who, "so long as the sea is calm . . . can discern movements in the depths of the sea in such a way that not even one of the creatures crosses his path unseen."[224]

When Diadochus considers immature the fundamental level of discernment simply between good and evil, he underscores the call to perfection. Otherwise, given the fallen state of human nature, Diadochus astutely observes that "one simply ends up seeking himself."[225] He presents this struggle in terms of wisdom, something accessible but only obtained if sought and granted. Once received, "the mind, impregnated, as it were, by the action of the Spirit, becomes something akin to a spring overflowing with love and joy."[226]

---

[223] GC 30.
[224] GC 26.
[225] See GC 96.
[226] GC 34.

The Third Stage—Teleoi *(The Perfect)*

The return to authentic humanity through arrival at restored likeness to God is not the end of the spiritual journey. Rather, it is the last preparation for mystical matrimony with God. The concept of "spiritual matrimony" is thoroughly scriptural, found throughout the Old Testament where God speaks of Israel in nuptial terms.[227] In the New Testament, under the New Covenant, Christ identifies himself as the divine Spouse to the church and to individual souls, each one his bride.[228] This was a common theme among the fathers of the East and West. Tertullian writes: "the flesh follows the soul which is now married to the Spirit, as part of the bridal offering, no longer servant of the soul, but of the Spirit."[229] Origen teaches: "Christ is the spouse to whom the soul is united in faith."[230] Cyril of Jerusalem says with more precision that after baptism, she who was a servant has received the Lord as her Spouse.[231] Dydimus the Blind echoes Cyril with "he who has created our soul takes her as spouse in the baptismal font."[232]

Diadochus's dedicates little attention to this doctrine. Since his is a practical theologian, he is more interested in providing counsel for the journey rather than spending more than a minimum amount of time elaborating on the goal. In GC 67 Diadochus lays out the path to such mystical union and describes the eschatological phenomenon:

> All of God's gifts are exceedingly beautiful and attain every benefit, but none of them moves and makes our heart to burn with love for his goodness as much as *theologia*. . . . It illumines our intellect in the fire of transformation and then brings it to enter into communion with those spirits that serve the Lord

---

[227] See Jer 2:20; Ezek 16; Hos 2; the entire book of Song of Songs.

[228] See Matt 9:15; 22:2; 26:1-13; Luke 12:36; Rev 19:7-10; 21:3.

[229] *De Anima*, 2.41; PL 2:720. Author's translation.

[230] *In gen hom* 10; PL 12:218. Author's translation.

[231] *De baptism* 10; PG 33:425.

[232] *De trinitate*; PG 33:692. Author's translation.

[see Heb 1:14]. Those of us, beloved, who have already been truly prepared for it desire this beautiful virtue, a thoroughly contemplative friend [to our soul], which achieves freedom from every worry, which, in the brilliance of indescribable light, nourishes the mind on the words of God. In a word, through the holy prophets the rational mind is united with divine Logos in an indissoluble communion, so that even among human beings—O wonder!—this godly bridesmaid [*nymphagōgos*] might harmonize the divinized voices which sing clearly of God's magnificence.

Theologia is also called *nymphagōga*.[233] The *nyhmphagōga* is the chaperone who guides the bride to the house of the groom and ultimately to his royal wedding chamber. Diadochus alludes to Psalm 45:14, The Royal Wedding Song, which says, "Dressed in brocades, the king's daughter is led to the king, with bridesmaids in her train." *Theologia* is this mediation that leads the soul to union with God and introduces it to his nuptial mysteries. For Diadochus, *theologia*, a sign of perfection, although always mystical, is never an end in itself. The end is divine nuptials and theology is the necessary means toward it. In GC 79 Diadochus quotes this psalm directly with regard to the soul as an intimate place where God and the human bride are alone together, outside of the enemy's reach.

Such is the goal. What follows is an exposition on the nature of this third stage.

"Just as wisdom and knowledge are gifts of the one Holy Spirit, so too are all divine gifts; nonetheless, each gift has its own operation."[234] The gifts serve to purify the intellect, the principal place of the Holy Spirit's operation in the third stage. In doing so, they bring peace and permit access to the "lamp of knowledge"[235]—which is Christ's spirit, incarnate wisdom. In other words, wisdom and knowledge are gifts of the Holy Spirit, each

---

[233] I have translated this word as "bridesmaid."
[234] GC 9.
[235] See GC 28.

with its distinctive operation. Knowledge aids in discerning between good and evil,[236] and is granted to the person who, after much prayer, has acquired a degree of *apatheia*.[237] Diadochus describes this *scientia amoris* from his own experience—although he writes as if it were something told to him by another:

> Someone from among those who love the Lord with unyielding resolve once told me the following: "Because I longed for conscious knowledge of the love of God, he who is Goodness itself granted me it; and ever since I have experienced the action of this sense with full certainty to such a degree that my soul was spurned on with joyful desire and ineffable love so that it quit my body to go with the Lord[238]—to the point of almost losing all awareness of this passing life."[239]

Similar to Saint Paul, our author describes the heights of mystical experience in radical terms. More than simply a description of the tension of wanting to be with the Lord to such an extent that he loses much more than a taste for this life, it is a description of mystical death. He includes the body as participant in this experience, which points to the eschatological dimension of this ecstasy and attributes an anticipatory value to this communication: "The joy that actually is produced in the soul and the body is a reliable reminder of incorruptible life."[240] The redeemed human person returns to his original integration and experiences—as opposed to merely tastes—the superabundance of glory that God pours into him. This eschatological anticipation is founded on ever-advancing love, which will never cease to have two objects: God and others. In the same chapter in which Diadochus describes the apex of union with God he includes its logical consequence

---

[236] See GC 6.
[237] See GC 9.
[238] See 2 Cor 12:2.
[239] GC 91.
[240] GC 25.

of love for enemies, thus underlining the inseparability of heaven and earth for the mystic undergoing glorifying transformation.[241]

The intimacy of such union prohibits the mystic from any exteriorization or speech about such experiences, lest he open the doors of the bathhouse, allowing all the warmth to escape.[242]

Wisdom, like knowledge an exclusively supernatural gift, is similar in attributes to knowledge.[243] Yet it not only permits speech of its own experience but also impels it. In other words, there is a charismatic element here lacking in knowledge. Whereas knowledge illumines through actions, wisdom illumines through the word and is granted only after much meditation on Sacred Scripture.[244] It is wisdom that educates the warrior's spiritual palate to intuit the goings on in the soul, to reject what is evil and to choose between better and best.[245]

Far above and beyond both these gifts is the gift of theology. Nothing short of theology makes the soul burn with love for God and only God could prepare and grant such a gift.[246] GC 67, as seen above, describes the consequences of this gift. Theology and knowledge never cohabitate to their fullness in the same person. Although the Gnostic may have attained a certain degree of contemplation and the theologian has experiential knowledge, the nature of each requires the totality of the person.[247]

Arrival at the third stage cancels out the balance between fear and love in which true love casts out all fear (1 John 4:19). "In those, however, who have been purified, there is perfect love. In such as they, there is not even a thought of fear, but never-ending fire and fusion of soul with God, by the working of the Holy Spirit; as it is said: my soul clings close to you, your right hand supports

---

[241] See GC 91.
[242] See GC 70.
[243] See GC 9.
[244] See GC 9.
[245] See GC 31.
[246] See GC 66.
[247] See GC 72.

me [Ps 63:8]."[248] This love is an interior fire. "Proper to a pure soul is . . . ardent love [*eros*] for the glory of the Lord. When the mind has these qualities, it measures itself with its own reason comparably to the judgment of that incorruptible tribunal."[249]

Diadochus echoes Saint Paul when describing this *eros* for God:

> One who loves God with the sense of the heart "is known by him" [1 Cor 8:3], because inasmuch as one receives the love of God, according to that measure he will dwell in the love of God. And from that moment onward, he comes to find himself immersed in such an ardent longing for the illumination of the intellect, penetrating even his bones, that he loses all awareness of himself and he is completely transformed by the love of God.[250]

As a result, such "fervor [is] granted to the heart by the Holy Spirit . . . [that] it arouses every part of the soul to long for God, not blown about outside one's heart but all through it delighting the entire person in charity and boundless joy."[251] Love and joy become "boundless" because the mystical death, the "second martyrdom,"[252] abolishes every boundary dividing the formerly fragmented senses, opening up the entire person to the utter simplicity of God. As a result, the mystic discovers his own totality. The encounter with divine Love "makes our soul burn with so great a love for God, that every part of the soul is ineffably united to the sweetness of this divine desire in an attitude of unending simplicity."[253] At the same time the intellect is so penetrated by the divine light that it is capable of seeing the light it has appropriated deep within the soul.[254] Diadochus goes on to say that,

---

[248] GC 16.
[249] GC 19.
[250] GC 14.
[251] GC 74.
[252] See GC 94.
[253] GC 34.
[254] See GC 40.

"in the moment in which someone is spurred on by God to such a degree of love, he is elevated beyond faith because when he reaches the very peaks of love, he now possesses him in the keen perception [*aisthēsis*] of his heart whom he first honored with faith."[255]

The penetrating warmth of this divine love engenders joyful, loving tears—a new quality of tears proportional to this stage.[256] And the intensified presence of the gifts of the Holy Spirit work to purify the intellect to such an extent that the soul finds itself in a state where the memory is liberated from every image.[257] "Living our whole life long gazing into the depths of our hearts with undying memory of God, we ought to live as blind men throughout this deceptive life. Thus proper to a truly spiritual philosophy is to clip the wings of ardent love for visible things."[258]

Arrival at the third stage is not without its dangers. Although unlikely, it is indeed possible for the warrior who has attained a degree of perfection to fall back into his old ways. This is not only because human nature is weakened from original sin but also because of God's respect for human freedom—even in its misuse.

> Further, one who has advanced to this degree God sometimes abandons to the devil's wickedness and the darkening of the intellect so that our freedom not be completely chained up by the bonds of grace—not only so that sin is defeated by his fight, but also because the person should continue to proceed into the spiritual trial. For whatever the disciple considers perfect in himself is actually an imperfection with respect to God's ambition which instructs us with a love that seeks to surpass its own achievements and climb to the top of the ladder that appeared to Jacob.[259]

---

[255] GC 91.
[256] See GC 73, 100.
[257] See GC 60.
[258] GC 56.
[259] GC 85.

Acquisition of such levels of purification and identity through grace makes the warrior possess the virtues and elements proper to this stage "as if by nature."[260] The term "stage" is not as determining or static as it might appear. Nor is achieving the heights of the third stage a common phenomenon. "This is so because no one still in the flesh can attain his perfection except the saints who make it to martyrdom and perfect confession."[261]

God's desire is to divinize his children.[262] And Diadochus has taught us the way to this goal, which, in turn, permits the celebration of divine nuptials. It entails loving and being loved and being transformed into divine love until such moment that we are "robed in divine love."[263] Only in such a state do we find our true selves.[264] And seeing ourselves as we are and as we ought to be, we are then capable of giving ourselves completely to the divine Spouse in one eternal matrimonial embrace, for which we were made and for which we long.

This Translation and Texts Consulted

I used Edouárd Des Places's critical edition of the Greek text for my own translation of all four works. I am unaware of any previously published English translations of *The Homily on the Ascension, The Catechesis,* and *The Vision.* Des Places offers a French translation of these works, and Pablo Argárate has published all four Diadochan works in Spanish.[265] A Latin translation of the *Homily* was published by Cardinal Angelo Mai in 1840.[266] Vincenzo Messana published an Italian translation of the *Gnostic Chapters,*[267]

---

[260] GC 95.

[261] GC 90.

[262] See Homily 6.

[263] Homily 6.

[264] See GC 80.

[265] *Diadoco de Fótice: Obras Completas* (Madrid: Editorial Ciudad Nueva, Biblioteca de Patrística, 1999).

[266] PG 65:1141–48.

[267] *Cento Considerazioni sulla Fede* (Rome: Città Nuova, 1978).

and K. Suso Frank published a German version of this work under the title *Gespür für Gott*.[268] Further, Francisco Torres, SJ, published a Latin translation of the *Gnostic Chapters* in 1570, which, upon first publication, justly won high praise for its style.[269] I know of two English translations of *Gnostic Chapters* prior to mine—one found in the *Philokalia*[270] and another fine work by the scholar Janet Rutherford, titled *One Hundred Practical Texts of Perception and Spiritual Discernment from Diadochos of Photikē*.[271] Although disparate, both are excellent translations.

If there exist two good English translations of this text, why a third, one might ask. The *Philokalia* translation is highly readable and follows Horace's advice to translators quite stringently:

> nec verbo verbum curabis reddere fidus
> interpres nec desilies imitator in artum,
> unde pedem proferre pudor vetet aut operis lex.[272]

Horace counsels the translator to get out of the all-too-comfortable rut of the word-for-word translation done in the name of fidelity to the text. The *Philokalia* translation succeeds in this and provides us with a literary—as opposed to a literal—translation, in certain parts. On the other hand, Rutherford's translation intentionally snubs Horace with the valid argument that the reader has a right to an adequate reflection of the original text and that the text's linguistic and grammatical integrity ought to be respected. Certainly there is room for both methods and the translators have attained their goals.

Given Diadochus's difficult style and my aversion to an adulterated translation, my goal is to provide the reader with a third

---

[268] K. Suso Frank, *Gespür für Gott* (Einsiedlen: Johannes Verlag, 1982).

[269] *De perfectione spirituali capita centum*, PG. 65:1162–1212.

[270] G. E. H. Palmer, Phillip Sherrard, and Kallistos Ware, trans., *Philokalia* (London: Faber and Faber, 1979).

[271] Janet Rutherford, *One Hundred Practical Texts of Perception and Spiritual Discernment from Diadochos of Photikē* (Belfast: Belfast Byzantine Texts and Translations, Institute of Byzantine Studies, 8, 2000).

[272] *Ars Poetica*, 133–34.

way. At the outset my proposed task was to offer a literal translation, faithful to the text but readable. Diadochus did not make it easy for me. His style is difficult; his vocabulary is rich, vast, and precise; and quite often his sentences are very long. I have taken it upon myself to shorten some of Diadochus's longer sentences, and where I have opted for something other than a word-for-word translation I offer explanations in the footnotes.

Whether I have achieved my goal is up to the reader. If someone can improve on my efforts that would be appreciated. I am, after all, a student of Greek, not a master. If, in spite of the deficiencies of my own work, someone finds spiritual food and grows in love for Christ through Diadochus's work, I would count it a blessing and my work worthwhile.

Discourses on Judgment and Spiritual Discernment

One Hundred Gnostic Chapters by Diadochus, Bishop of Photikē in Epiros

The first definition: Faith: an impassible[1] consideration of God.

The second definition: Hope: an emigration[2] of the intellect in love, moving toward those things that await us.

The third definition: Patience: to steadfastly persevere in seeing with the eyes of the mind the invisible as well as the visible.

Fourth definition: Detachment from riches[3]: to want to possess nothing with as much desire as those who want to possess.

Fifth definition: Knowledge: unawareness of oneself[4] in the ecstasy of God.

Sixth definition: Humility: to forget constantly your successes.

Seventh definition: Meekness: a strong longing not to get angry.

---

[1] Or "passionless."

[2] "Emigration," lit. "going abroad." "Abandonment" also provides a valid translation in the sense of leaving behind worldly banalities, of being *auf dem Weg* in a *status viatoris* that is proper to the virtue of hope.

[3] Lit. "freedom from avarice."

[4] The phrase our author uses means literally "not to know oneself" or "to be unaware of oneself."

Eighth definition: Purity: to sense continually being united to God.

Ninth definition: Charity: to grow in friendship toward those who insult us.

Tenth definition: Complete transformation: reveling[5] in God's delight while joyfully considering the gloom[6] of death.

---

[5] Diadochus uses a word that has a wanton, reckless, even licentious meaning.

[6] *Stugnos*: our author uses a term frequently associated with the concept of Greek Hades.

Discourses on Judgment and Spiritual Discernment by Diadochus, Bishop of Photikē in Epiros

Knowledge necessary to advance toward perfection, under guidance of the Lord, which has been manifest to us so that each of us bring to fruition the seed of the word, according to the example of the liberating parable.[7]

Chapters

1. All spiritual contemplation, brothers, should be guided by faith, hope, and charity—but above all by charity.[8] The first two teach us to despise visible goods, but charity unites the soul to the very virtues of God, so that, by way of intellectual sense[9] it can follow the footprints[10] of the Invisible One.

---

[7] See Matt 13:18-23.

[8] See 1 Cor 13:13.

[9] *Aisthēsis noera.*

[10] The verb is lit. "to track" and comes from tracking used in hunting. For Diadochus the task of each Christian is to follow the traces that lead to God. These are first perceived through the ever refined "sense." The hunting metaphor was first used by Plato, "following the tracks of truth" (*Meno*, 1235–49), as well as by Sophocles, Polyaenus (*Anthologia Graeca*, 368 [lyr.]), Plutarch (*Pompeius*, 27), and up to our own time in Francis Thompson's famous poem "The Hound of Heaven."

2. Only God is good by nature.[11] But through moral effort, a person, too, can become good, transforming himself by way of the essential Good[12] into that which he is not, when the soul, striving for the Good, becomes God[13] inasmuch his faculty (moved by Him), desires it. For it is written: *be merciful as your heavenly Father is merciful.*[14]

3. Evil is not in nature nor is anyone evil by nature, since God made nothing evil.[15] But when in the concupiscence of heart someone gives shape to that which is not in reality, then precisely that which he desires begins to exist. Therefore, we must always take care to turn our attention away from an evil disposition by clinging to the memory of God. The nature of the good is stronger than our tendency to evil. For one is, while the other, unless made to be through action, is not.[16]

4. All of us are [made] according to the image of God; but only those who through great love have enslaved their own freedom to God are in his likeness.[17] When we no longer belong to our-

---

[11] See Luke 18:19. "Why do you call me 'good'? No one is good but God alone." This allusion seems to have escaped Des Places, et al.

[12] Note that it is by way of divine Goodness that humans reach this transformation—but not without their own striving. Diadochus manifests his balanced and respectful vision of anthropology and divinity in which one never imposes on or detracts from the other. Nonetheless, our moral acts are not done in a vacuum—when brought about in cooperation with grace they result in a greater "likeness" to the One in whose "image" we were made. Further, the reference to Luke 6:36 indicates the qualities of those acts that most bring about this transformation into God: mercy and compassion.

[13] This theme, the fulfillment of Diadochus's spiritual itinerary, is more explicit: "We are not transformed into what we were, but renewed with glory by the transformation into what we were not" (*Homily on the Ascension of our Lord Jesus Christ*, 4).

[14] See Luke 6:36.

[15] See Gen 1:31.

[16] Diadochus counters the Messalian belief of substantial evil yet admits the power of moral evil, which is a type of anti-creation, bringing about not only what does not exist but that which corrupts what already exists.

[17] See Rom 5:10; 2 Cor 5:18-19. Charity differentiates likeness from image. Since image is impressed on the person through the received nature, it is charity that expresses divine life within the person.

selves, then we are similar to him who has reconciled us to himself through love. No one will attain to this state if he does not convince his soul to be unmoved by the facile human glory[18] of this life.

5. Freedom is the ability of the rational[19] soul to move swiftly toward whatever it wants. Let us persuade it then to be readily disposed for the good, so that we always wipe away the memory of evil through good thoughts.

6. The light of true knowledge[20] is to discern infallibly good and evil. Thus the road of righteousness leads the mind to the Sun of Righteousness[21] and where it is inducted into the boundless illumination of knowledge, so that hereafter it searches boldly for love. Therefore, with the soul[22] freed of anger, we must wrest what is good from those who dare to abuse it, since holy zeal, not hatred,[23] wins out[24] through admonishment of their faults.[25]

7. Spiritual discourse brings the intellectual sense to full measure. It comes from God borne by the power of love; therefore our mind is not belabored and perseveres in its examination[26] of theology. Thus it does not suffer the impoverishment that disquiet

---

[18] The *Philokalia*'s (hereafter called P) translation "false glitter" seems a bit too free, while a direct translation of *eukolon doxan* is easily understood.

[19] P translates *logikes* as "deiform."

[20] *Phōs gnōseos alēthinēs*—"the light of true knowledge," Diadochus's own term meaning the place where doctrine and praxis meet.

[21] Mal 3:20.

[22] P says "incensive power."

[23] P's "aspiration for holiness," although more intelligible, does not reflect *ho tēs eusebeias zelos*.

[24] Lit. "gains the victory." P does not translate the word *to nikos* ("victory"), while Messana's Italian translation (hereafter called M) adds the concept of singing victory "canta vittoria." S, in his turn makes of it something altogether different with "Überredung zum Sieg" reflecting the idea of convincing someone to victory.

[25] The Spanish translation by Argárate (A) says merely *persuadiendo* and Des Places's French translation (hereafter called D) says *persuasion*, which does not say enough, while M neglects to translate "faults." Des Places seems to faithfully mirror Torres's sixteenth-century Latin translation (T).

[26] Lit. "in its movements," although there are many possibilities with this word.

brings,[27] because through its contemplations it is filled in proportion to the measure of desire in its exercise of charity.[28] It is always better to await the illumination of faith, energized by love, which equips us to speak, since nothing is more miserable than a Godless mind philosophizing about God.

8. The unenlightened should not undertake spiritual contemplation, and much less should one[29] begin to speak while the light of the Holy Spirit—in his kindness— comes upon him. For where there is poverty, ignorance abounds, but where there are riches, speech is impossible. The soul intoxicated by the charity of God wants to enjoy the glory of the Lord with stilled voice. Therefore, we have to keep the balance in our activity if we are to begin to speak about God. On the one hand, this balance makes our words of praise satisfying.[30] On the other hand, abundance of illumination nourishes the faith of him who speaks in faith, so that he who teaches may first enjoy the fruits of knowledge through love. It is the working farmer who has the first claim on any crop that is harvested.[31]

9. Just as wisdom and knowledge are gifts of the one Holy Spirit, so too are all divine gifts; nonetheless, each gift has its own operation. That is why the Apostle testifies that to one is given the gift of wisdom, to another knowledge according to the Holy

---

[27] P misses the mark translating it thus: "it does not suffer then from the emptiness which produces a state of anxiety"; rather it seems clear, according our author, that it is precisely anxiety and disquiet that impoverish the soul.

[28] Lit. "energy of love."

[29] D and A suddenly make the subject the first person plural, while the text indicates the third-person singular.

[30] Instead of "satisfaction," P uses "harmony" and M seems to stray even further translating it as *stilo* (style). A has it as *belleza* (beauty), and S writes *Freude* (joy). In spite of the many possibilities offered, the word *charizetai* carries with it a sense of indulgence, pleasure, or satisfaction. Frank seems to translate this sentence quite freely saying, *die besondere Freude über das herrliche Wort* ("the special joy of the glorious word"). P, M, and A all insert the word "God" into this clause, while D seems to have stayed closer to the Greek text, translating it as *Cette mesure nous vaut je ne sais quelle beauté de discourse glorieux.*

[31] See 2 Tim 2:6.

Spirit.[32] Indeed, knowledge unites the person to God by experience,[33] yet it does not move the soul to speak of what has occurred. Therefore, some of them who are philosophers[34] in solitary life have been illumined by such spiritual knowledge yet never utter divine words.[35] Wisdom, on the contrary, when granted to someone together with knowledge in fear—which rarely occurs—manifests the same operations as knowledge, since, on the one hand, knowledge illumines through actions, while the other [wisdom] illuminates through the word. But knowledge is brought about by prayer and perfect quiet in complete detachment, while wisdom comes through humble[36] meditation[37] of God's word and, foremost, thanks to God's grace.

10. When the irascible part of the soul is stirred against the passions, remember[38] that it is time for silence—the hour of battle. But upon seeing that the upheaval is passing, be it through prayer or almsgiving, then it is the moment to let yourself be drawn by the ardent love[39] of God's words, affixing the wings of your mind to humility.[40] For if a person does not humble himself exceedingly, he will never be able to speak of God's greatness.[41]

---

[32] 1 Cor 12:8.

[33] Knowledge, for our author, is something far removed from aggregates of information. It is a binding experience, the beginning of transformation. See GC 91.

[34] For the fathers, the true philosopher is the one consecrated to seeking true Wisdom, God alone.

[35] A translates *sin llegar a hablar de Dios* ("without coming to speak about God"), although to his credit he gives a literal translation in his footnote. He seems to be following D's translation. M translates *senza venire mai a svelare cio che Dio rivela* ("without coming to reveal what God has revealed").

[36] Lit. "without vainglory."

[37] *Meletē* means "exercise" but with the fathers it took upon itself the sense of spiritual exercise—meditation.

[38] Lit. "it is necessary to recognize."

[39] *Eros*, D finds a literary allusion to Plato's *Eros pandemos* (p. 58).

[40] Lit. "lowliness of mind."

[41] Diadochus presents us with the paradox of lowering oneself as the prerequisite of ascent: lowliness of mind must precede spiritual flight; humility must precede the experience of God's greatness.

11. Spiritual discourse always protects the soul from vainglory, bestowing light on every part of her so that she does not feel the need of human praise. Therefore, it also preserves the mind from useless imagination, transforming it into the love of God.[42] Conversing according to worldly wisdom, on the contrary, always arouses the love of vainglory. And given that it cannot grant the benefits of spiritual experience, it offers to those who practice it the satisfaction of praise—product of other vain men. Thus, in the proper state we will know how faultlessly to recognize[43] the word of God, if we spend hours in untroubled silence, not speaking and in the fervent memory of God.

12. He who loves himself cannot love God, but he who does not love himself on account of the immeasurable riches of God's love, loves God indeed.[44] Therefore, never seek such glory for yourself, but for God alone. He who loves himself, seeks his own glory, while he who loves God, seeks the glory of the One who created him. It is characteristic of a spiritually sensitive soul enamored of God to seek his glory alone in all the commandments he observes, for such a soul as this finds joy in lowliness. Glory is fitting to God because of his majesty, but to man, lowliness. For it is precisely through humility that we take God as our dwelling place.[45] Indeed, if we proceed in this way, we too, along with Saint John the Baptist, will rejoice in the glory of the Lord and begin to cry out: He must increase, and I must decrease.[46]

13. I know of a man[47] who loves God so much that his inability to love him more is his greatest affliction. His incessantly ardent

---

[42] *Theosis* requires a total transformation, fruit of the encounter with God; see GC 14 and 67, and *Homily* 6.

[43] P says "speak about," while M says *cogliere* ("receive").

[44] See Eph 2:6.

[45] Frank's German translation (F) understands this word as *vertraut werden* ("to be married to"), A has *lleguemos a la intimidad* ("come to intimacy with . . ."), D says *pour devenir par ce moyen le familier de Dieu* ("to become familiar with"), P makes of this verb "unite to," while M's translation is *entrare in intimo rapporto con Dio* ("to enter into an intimate relationship with God").

[46] See John 3:30.

[47] Diadochus is referring to himself.

desire is that God be glorified in himself while he should be as nothing. This man does not know who he is,[48] even amid words of praises [about him]; for in his great longing for lowliness he never considers his own rank, but serves God according to priestly custom. In his profound desire to love God, he robs himself of the very memory of his rank in the abyss of his love for God. Any cause for boasting he conceals with a spirit of humility, for in his own mind, he considers himself as nothing more than a useless servant. His longing for lowliness makes his rank foreign to him. So should we act, fleeing every honor and glory for the "overabundant riches"[49] of the love of the Lord who has so loved us.

14. The one who loves God with the sense of the heart "is known by him,"[50] because inasmuch as one receives the love of God, according to that measure he will dwell in the love of God. And from that moment onward, he comes to find himself immersed in such an ardent longing for the illumination of the intellect, penetrating even his bones, that he loses all awareness of himself and is completely transformed by the love of God. Such a one is present and absent in this life. He has his body for a dwelling place, but vacates it through love. He relentlessly moves toward God in his soul. Once he has transcended his self-love through love for God, his heart becomes consumed in the fire of love and clings to God with unyielding desire. "If we seem out of our senses it was for God; but if we are being reasonable now, it is for your sake."[51]

15. When one begins to perceive the riches of God's love, then he begins to love his neighbor in the spiritual sense. This is the love of which all the Scriptures speak. Since friendship according to the flesh is not founded on the spiritual sense, upon encountering some flimsy pretext it dissolves. It may occur that irritations arise for the soul under God's influence, but the bond of love is

---

[48] See how definition 5 describes knowledge as being lost in God through ecstasy.

[49] Eph 2:7.

[50] 1 Cor 8:3.

[51] 2 Cor 5:13. At the beginning of this quote P inserts "Paul writes."

not broken; rather, renewed with fervent love for God, she invokes goodness yet again and, with ever more haste and deeper joy, loves her neighbor—yes, even one who has gravely insulted and hurt her. Bitterness of the quarrel is completely consumed by God's sweetness.

16. No one can love God with all his heart, if he does not fear God with all his heart, because only the purified soul, tamed by the influence of this fear as it were, is capable of yielding to love's action. But he will not completely achieve the fear of God just described, if he does not first relinquish every mundane worry. When the mind reaches this level of quiet[52] and total freedom of such worry, then the fear of God comes to put the mind in travail. It seeks to scour it of the thick, earthy layers that cover it, and lead it to a higher love of God's goodness in the deepest sense.

Therefore, the fear corresponding to those who are still being purified is accompanied by imperfect love. Perfect love, on the contrary, is had by those who are purified already, in whom there is no more fear. It is said, *perfect love casts out fear.*[53] The one and the other are found only in the righteous who are under the influence of the Holy Spirit and put virtues into practice. It is for that reason that it says somewhere: *Fear Yahweh, you his holy ones: those who fear him, lack nothing,*[54] and in another place: *Love Yahweh, all you devout*[55]; so that we clearly understand that in the righteous who are still being purified, there is a mediocre love, as has been said. In those, however, who have been purified, there is perfect love. In such as they, there is not even a thought of fear, but never-ending fire and fusion of soul with God, by the working of the Holy Spirit; as it is said: *closely my soul clings to you, your right hand holds me fast.*[56]

17. Just as wounds occur on the body and when left unattended without the least consideration do not feel the remedy that the

---

[52] *Hēsuchia.*
[53] 1 John 4:18.
[54] Ps 34:9.
[55] Ps 31:23.
[56] Ps 63:8.

doctors apply, but once they are cleaned, they feel the remedy bringing them to quick recovery; so too with the soul. Inasmuch as it is uncared for and completely covered with the leprosy of the love of pleasure, it cannot feel fear of God even though it is continuously forewarned about God's terrible and powerful judgment.[57] But once it begins to be purified thanks to much great attention, it then feels the burning fear of God to be a true life-remedy, thanks to the effect of its reproaches[58] amid the fire of impassibility. Thereafter, it is partially purified, anticipating a perfect purification, growing in charity to the same degree in which it diminishes in fear, in order to arrive at perfect love, in which, as it has been said, there is no fear but rather complete impassibility wrought by God's glory. May our supreme boast be the boast of unceasing fear of God[59] and the love which is the fullness of the law[60] of perfection in Christ.

18. A soul not yet liberated from worldly concerns cannot truly love God nor despise the devil as is fitting, because he wears life's worries like a burdensome shroud. Thus his mind is incapable of recognizing its own tribunal[61] in order to examine his own verdict with certainty. Therefore it is useless for him to retire from the world.

19. Proper to a pure soul is to speak[62] without envy, zeal without malice, unyielding and ardent love[63] for the glory of the Lord.[64] When the mind has these qualities, it measures itself with its own reason comparably to the judgment of that incorruptible tribunal.

---

[57] A, D *tribunal* and M uses *tribunale*.

[58] P adds "in the conscience."

[59] P translates this as "let us rejoice endlessly in our fear of God," but *kauchema* means a boast or vaunt, not rejoicing. Perhaps he follows D's lead who translates it as *pour obtenir la joie des joie sans fin*, which is quite similar.

[60] See Rom 13:10.

[61] Lit. "court of justice."

[62] Lit. "a word."

[63] *Eros* for God is the way to purity of heart!

[64] See 1 Cor 2:8.

20. Faith without works and faithless works will both be tried and condemned.[65] Therefore it is necessary that the believer offer the Lord a faith proven by actions.[66] Our father Abraham's faith would not have declared him righteous if he had not offered its fruit, his son.[67]

21. He who loves God truly believes and carries out works with devotion. But he who merely believes without living in charity does not in fact have the faith he seems to have. He believes but with a superficial mind, and so he is not moved to act by love's burden of glory.[68] *Faith strengthened by love*[69] is the pinnacle of the virtues.

22. When scrutinized the abyss of faith swells. But if it is approached with a simple disposition, it is calmed. The depths of faith are like Lethe, water that makes us forget all evil. The depths of faith do not tolerate being made an object of curiosity. So let us sail then upon these waters with simple thoughts in order to reach the port of God's will.[70]

23. No one can truly love or believe if he does not have himself as his own accuser. Thus, when our conscience is bothered by reproach, the mind is no longer permitted to sense the aroma of supernatural goods, rather it is quickly divided by doubts.[71] On the one hand, given its past experience it wants to reach out

---

[65] The word *apodokimazō* means lit. "rejected upon scrutiny by trial," yet P says simply "condemned," as does F (*verurteilt*). D says *seron réprouvées*, as does A, *serán reprobadas*, while M has it as merely *biasimate* ("charged" or "blamed").

[66] A and M, probably following D ascribe Titus 2:10 as the scriptural allusion here but there does not seem to be any relationship. F makes no such assertion. On the other hand, Jas 2:14-26 is clearly the source of inspiration for Saint Diadochus: *Faith is like that: if good works do not go with it, it is quite dead.* . . .

[67] See Gen 22; Rom 4:3.

[68] See 2 Cor 4:17.

[69] See Gal 5:6.

[70] See Ps 106:30.

[71] The word for doubt or uncertainty (*amphibolia*) comes from the verb "to be attacked on both sides"—a graphic description of what Diadochus is about to describe in this discourse.

fervently for the faith; but on the other hand, its sense of the heart can no longer receive it with love since the conscience pricks it with many reproaches, as I mentioned before. But when we have been purified through a more fervent attention[72] we will obtain what we desire with an even greater experience of God.

24. Just as the bodily senses spur us on with a sort of violence toward that which seems beautiful, so too the sense of the mind is in the habit of guiding us toward invisible goods[73] once it has tasted divine goodness.[74] Since everything aspires[75] to what is related to it,[76] the soul, inasmuch as it is immaterial, aspires to heavenly goods; while the body, a clump of soil, desires earthly sustenance. So without faltering we will achieve an immaterial experience if we endeavor to mitigate[77] what is material.

25. The exercise[78] of divine knowledge itself teaches us that there is only one natural sense in the soul, henceforth divided into two operations on account of Adam's disobedience. And on the other hand there is a single,[79] simple sense produced in her by the Holy Spirit, which no one can know except those who have willingly detached themselves from the goods of this life[80] in hopes of future goods and whose self-mastery makes bodily

---

[72] Torres's Latin translation says "prayer and attention," since the Greek words for these terms are quite similar and easily confused. In fact, manuscripts seem to vary between these two words. The SCh Greek text says *Prosochē* ("attention").

[73] *Agatha*—P translates this as "blessings."

[74] See Ps 33:9.

[75] Lit. "totally aspires."

[76] F seems to add to the text with his translation: *was ihm entspricht und nächtverwandt ist*, ("what corresponds to him and is closely related to him").

[77] *Leptunō*, lit. "to thresh, to thin." P translates this as "refine," which does not express the exigency of the word, while D has it as *exténuons* ("exhaust"), while A and F concur respectively with *debilitamos* and *abschwächen* ("weaken") and M makes it *andiamo eliminando* ("eliminate"). In any case, it seems Diadochus presents us with an anomaly in the sense that his normally positive teaching on the value of sense experience suddenly takes a turn for the pejorative.

[78] P translates this "once it has been awakened."

[79] M neglects this word.

[80] P adds the word "corruptible," which does not appear in the Greek text.

attractions to die off.[81] In them alone, thanks to their detachment, can the mind exercise at full strength so as to perceive God's ineffable blessings. As a result it transmits its own share of joy even to the body, in proportion to its progress, exulting without ceasing in its full confession of love.[82] *My heart,* he says, *places its trust in him; I have been helped, my flesh has flourished once again, I thank him with all my heart.*[83] The joy that actually is produced in the soul and the body is a reliable reminder of incorruptible life.

26. Warriors should always keep custody of their thoughts so that the mind can discern the thoughts that pass through it and store in the memory banks those that are good and come from God, while casting out of nature's storage all those that are perverse[84] or diabolical. Therefore, so long as the sea is calm fishermen can discern movements in the depths of the sea in such a way that not even one of the creatures crosses his path unseen. But when it[85] is stirred up by the winds, what was visible in the joy[86] of calm is now hidden under gloomy waves. From this we see how futile are angler's genius and talent when running up against the deceits of the deep.[87] And this is exactly what happens to the contemplative mind, above all when the depths of the soul are stirred up by unjust anger.

27. To only a very few is it given to know all of their falls, indeed to those whose mind is never torn away from the memory of God. Our physical eyes, when healthy, can see everything—even the smallest of gnats and mosquitoes flying about in the air. But when they are covered by[88] some tumor or have become clouded and

---

[81] A says *debilitan* ("weaken") as does F (*entkräften*), while M's version seems weaker still, *non estenua* (to not prolong). P's "wither away" is acceptable.

[82] See Ps 41:5.

[83] Ps 28:7.

[84] *Skaios,* lit. "on the left side," as in Latin, *sinister* took upon itself a pejorative shade.

[85] F, M, P insert "the sea."

[86] Lit. "smile."

[87] P omits the second clause in this sentence.

[88] P omits this verb.

some large object is put before them,[89] they see it dimly, while little things go unperceived by the eye.[90] So too the soul; if it, by way of its attention, overcomes the blindness which comes from loving the world, then it will consider even its minor falls as very grave, thus producing[91] continually tears upon tears with much gratitude. *The just, so it says, will confess your name.*[92] But on the contrary, if he continues in his worldly attitude and were he to murder *someone or do something deserving of harsh punishment, he will* reckon it only slightly. With regard to his other faults, he is incapable of recognizing them and often considers them good actions. Indeed, this wretch is not embarrassed fervently to defend them.

28. The Holy Spirit alone purifies the mind. For if the strong man does not enter and strip the thief of what he has taken, the spoils will never be restored.[93] Therefore, it is necessary to use every means possible—especially peace of soul—so that the Holy Spirit might rest and, in this way, we will have the light of knowledge manifest[94] within us. With undying brightness in the treasury[95] of the soul, not only are those terrible and dark attacks exposed, but they are also very much weakened upon being rebuked[96] by that holy and glorious light. That is why the Apostle says, *do not extinguish the Spirit,*[97] which means, do not sadden the goodness of the Holy Spirit through evil deeds or words, lest you be deprived of that triumphant light. For the Eternal Giver of Life[98] is not

---

[89] P omits this clause.

[90] Lit. "by the sense of the eyes."

[91] D adds *á Dieu* ("to God") in brackets and A and M follow suit.

[92] Ps 140:14.

[93] See Matt 12:29. D is alone in not seeing this scriptural allusion.

[94] A, D, F, and M all concur with "burning," but that seems to be more of an interpretation of the verb *phainomai* than a translation.

[95] P's "inner shrine" seems to be an embellishment on a rather mundane word, *támieiov.*

[96] P seems to consolidate the two *katádeloi* ("manifest") and *elenchō* ("to lay evidence down against" or "rebuke").

[97] 1 Thess 5:19.

[98] *Zōopoion,* the classical title given to the Holy Spirit in the Nicean-Constantinople Symbol.

extinguished, rather he grieves, that is, he distances himself, thus leaving the mind in darkness dark and bereft of the light of knowledge.

29. The soul has only one natural sense, as I said,[99] and the five senses are distinguished according to the needs of the body; so teaches us the benevolent Holy Spirit of God. Nonetheless, on account of the fall[100] through disobedience, this one sense of the soul is distanced from the soul in its movements. Therefore, one part of it is dragged about by the passions, which is why we experience pleasure in the good things of this life; but the other part is often motivated by rational and spiritual delights when we practice moderation, which is why our mind is urged on toward those heavenly beauties when we live according to wisdom. If we learn to persevere in our disdain for worldly goods, we will be able to conjoin the earthly longings[101] of our soul to this disposition of the mind by way of communion with the Holy Spirit who makes this possible for us.[102] If his divinity does not illumine the treasures of our heart sufficiently, we will not be able to enjoy what is good with an undivided sense, that is, with an integral disposition.

30. The sense of the mind[103] has a precise taste for the things it discerns. Just as our corporal sense of taste flawlessly distinguishes between good and bad tastes when we are healthy and we are therefore drawn to good things, so too, when our mind starts to move about freely and without much worry, it is capable of feeling the wealth of divine consolation without ever being dragged here and there[104] by anything that could oppose it.[105] As the body tastes earthly sweetness and has a sure sense for it, so too the mind can infallibly recognize the Holy Spirit's consolation

---

[99] GC 25.

[100] D seems to have a typographical error, translating *olisthon* ("slip") as *plissement* (French for "wrinkle") rather than *glissement* ("slip").

[101] It is important to note that Saint Diadochus does not propose a repression of human longings, but to channel them toward their highest end.

[102] *Oikonomeō*—lit. "to arrange," "order," or "manage."

[103] *Aisthēsis noos.*

[104] P embellishes saying, "and is never led astray by any illusion of grace."

[105] P translates this as "the devil."

far above those of the flesh: *Taste*, it is said, *and see that the Lord is good.*[106] Through the exercise of love, the mind retains the memory of this taste, infallibly discerning the best things and choosing them, as the Saint says: *my prayer is that your love for each other may continually increase and never stop growing in your knowledge and deepening your sense,*[107] *so that you can always recognize what is best.*[108]

31. When our mind begins to feel the consolation of the Holy Spirit, then too Satan begins sweetly to lull[109] during the night's rest, when one is just starting to fall into a light sleep. But if the mind is recollected and perseveres in keeping the fervent memory of the Holy Name of Jesus, it will take strength from that holy and glorious Name[110] using it as a weapon against deception. Thereafter, the impostor leaves off his deceit and throws himself into waging open war against the soul. In this way the mind progresses more in its experience of discernment by recognizing the wiles of the evil one.

32. Good consolation[111] is brought about when the body is fully awake or even when it begins to feel sleep coming on, when one has bonded himself to [God's] love through the fervent memory of his Name. False consolation, on the other hand, is, as I have said, always produced when the warrior enters into light sleep, half forgetful of God. Thus, the first type comes from God who manifestly exhorts the souls of the warriors to a great outpouring of reverential love, whereas the other type, accustomed to influencing the soul with winds of deceit, attempts to rob the healthy

---

[106] Ps 33:9.

[107] *Aisthēsis*.

[108] Phil 1:9-10.

[109] D and M concur with the verb "console," but Diadochus takes pains to distinguish the diabolical deceits from divine consolations through the word *heduphanai*, which bears a more saccharine meaning than consolation, hence my option for "sweetly lull." P's version, "importune the soul with sweet deception," is definitely more verbose but stays more faithful to our author's original meaning. F qualifies his use of *Trösten* ("console") by adding *mit einem Gefühl, das angenehm erscheint*, "with a feeling that seems pleasant."

[110] P omits this clause.

[111] P translates *agathē paraklēsis* as "experience of grace."

mind of its experience of the memory of God while the body sleeps. But if the mind maintains the attentive memory of the Lord Jesus, as I mentioned, the enemy's apparently pleasant and mild breeze dissipates, and it then joyfully leaps into battle with its second weapon after grace: the confidence that comes from experience.

33. If the soul is set aflame for the love of God through an unambiguous and unimagined movement as if borne bodily into the ineffable depths of this love—as I have already said—either keeping vigil or falling asleep and, by work of holy grace, thinks of nothing else than that toward which it is moving, we should know that this is the action of the Holy Spirit. (Completely mollified by that ineffable sweetness, it is incapable of thinking of anything else—it enjoys ceaseless bliss.) But if the mind finds itself under the influence of doubt or conceives a filthy thought, even if it has employed the Holy Name in order to repel evil and not solely for love of God, then one must conclude that this consolation comes from the seducer under the appearance of joy. This joy is totally disordered and amorphous, coming from the enemy who wants to make the mind fall into adultery.[112] When [the enemy] sees the mind wholly trusting itself in the experience of its own sense, then, as I have said, he solicits the soul with certain apparently good consolations so that, divided by this vain and soothing sweetness, she is not able to penetrate this cunning union which deceives it. Therefore, we will recognize the spirit of truth and the spirit of illusion. Thus it is impossible that someone enjoy the taste in his interior sense of the divine goodness or sensibly experience the bitterness of the demons if he is not totally convinced that grace has taken up its dwelling place in the depths of his mind, while the evil spirits dwell around in the area of the heart; and the demons do not want that this be believed in any way by men, knowing that otherwise the mind would arm itself with the memory of God.

34. One thing is the natural love of the soul; another thing is that which comes about from the Holy Spirit. The first is moved

---

[112] F translates *moicheuō* as Untreue ("unfaithful").

in proportion to our will, through our desire.[113] Thus it is easily overcome[114] and carried off as plunder[115] by evil spirits when we fail to exercise fortitude in our endeavors. The other makes our soul burn with so great a love for God that every part of the soul is ineffably united to the sweetness of this divine desire in an attitude of unending simplicity. The mind, impregnated, as it were, by the action of the Spirit, becomes something akin to a spring overflowing with love and joy.

35. Just as when the sea is rough but by nature calms whenever oil is thrown onto it since its spray yields to oil,[116] so too, when our soul swells[117] by the kindness of the Holy Spirit, it is sweetly lulled to rest. Thus, it joyfully submits to the impassible and ineffable kindness which overshadows it,[118] as the Saint says: *My soul, be at rest in God alone.*[119] Thus, regardless of the amount of vexations the devil exerts upon the soul, it remains unperturbed and full of joy. One's soul arrives at this state and perseveres in it if it is continuously assuaged by the fear of God. Indeed, fear of the Lord Jesus brings about a certain purification in his warriors, *since the fear of the Lord is pure, enduring forever.*[120]

36. Let no one, upon hearing of the mind's perceptive faculty, expect the glory of God to appear to him visibly. We maintain, however, that when the soul senses, it is purified by the ineffable taste of divine consolation, yet nothing visible appears to it, because for now we walk by faith[121] and not by sight as the blessed Paul says. If a light or a fiery figure appears to any of the warriors, do not accept such a vision. This is a patent deception of the enemy. Many have suffered this through ignorance and have

---

[113] M has it as *è suscitato dalla nostra volonta secondo che comporta la sua natura.*

[114] Rutherford's very literal English translation (R) omits this word.

[115] P adds *and perverted.*

[116] P seems to paraphrase this.

[117] A translates this loosely as *ungida* (anointed).

[118] See Luke 1:35.

[119] Ps 62:6.

[120] Ps 19:10.

[121] See 2 Cor 5:7.

wandered from the path of truth. But we know that as long as we dwell in this corruptible body we are exiled from God.[122] That is to say, we cannot see him visibly—neither Him nor any of his heavenly wonders.

37. Dreams that reveal to the soul the love of God are sure indicators of a healthy soul. That is why they do not go from one image to another, nor do they frighten the senses, nor do they sneer or suddenly show a somber expression;[123] but rather they approach the soul completely reasonably, heaping upon[124] it spiritual delight. Therefore, even after the body has awakened, the soul seeks the joy of the dream with great desire. Demonic fantasies, on the other hand, are completely the opposite: they do not keep the same image and they do not manifest themselves in a consistent form for long.[125] This they do not willingly do, for in their deceit they only borrow such forms and cannot resist for long. They begin to scream and make lots of threats, often taking the form of soldiers, at times playing on[126] the soul with their shrieks. However, when the mind is purified it recognizes them and even in its dreaming it awakens the body. Other times it delights at having discovered the deceit. Therefore, confuting them over and over again in the same dream, it sparks his fury. It could even be that good dreams do not bring joy to the soul, but produce sweet sorrow and painless tears. This occurs when one has progressed much in lowliness of mind.

38. We have discussed the distinction between good and worthless dreams based on what we have heard from those with experience. But in our opinion it requires exercise of great virtue to not be led on by any such forms. For dreams are almost always

---

[122] See 2 Cor 5:6.

[123] P and R translate this as "threaten."

[124] Lit. "loading it down with," although A, D, F, and P all have a variation of "filling it with," which might be more pleasing to modern ears but does not reflect the verb.

[125] A adds sin causar turbación ("without causing anxiety").

[126] Lit. "plucking" as in playing on a harp. For some reason A, D, F, M, and P all want to translate this as "deafening."

nothing more than vague thoughts or the forms of errant thoughts or, as I have said, the mockery of devils. But even if God's goodness should send down a vision to us and yet we were never to accept it, our much longed for[127] Lord Jesus Christ would not be angry with us on that account, because he knows we come to this on account of diabolical deceptions. The discernment mentioned above is accurate, yet it happens that the soul could become sullied and imperceptibly taken hold of—and to my judgment, no one is exempt of this—and thus end up losing all traces of precise discernment and judging to be good those things [dreams] that are not.

39. Let us take the example of a servant called at night by his master who had been abroad yet now stands at the enclosure of the house. The servant absolutely refused to open the doors to his master out of fear of being fooled by a similar voice to hand over all the goods entrusted by the master. When day came, not only was his master not upset with him, rather he deemed his servant worthy of much praise because he took the master's voice for deception and did not want to lose any of his goods.[128]

40. When the intellect begins habitually to be activated by divine light, it becomes completely luminous even to the degree that it sees the abundance of its own light, and of this there is no doubt.[129] This occurs when the power of the soul achieves dominion over the passions. But Paul the Divine clearly teaches us that whatever appears, regardless of the form—be it light or fire—is a connivance of the enemy who changes himself into an angel of light.[130] One does not then take up the ascetical life with such hopes as this: that Satan not find the soul prime for picking; but rather that we come to love God alone with conviction and all the sense of our heart, which is to love God with all our heart, with

---

[127] *Polupothetos*—common title for Christ.

[128] See GC 84.

[129] Probably inspired by Evagrius (*Praktikos* 1.36; PG 40:1232A). This teaching would later influence the hesychast movement of the fourteenth century.

[130] See 2 Cor 11:14.

all our soul and with all our mind.[131] Whoever is moved by God
to this is exiled from the world even as he continues to live in the
world.

41. Obedience is known to be the foremost of all the founda-
tional virtues, since it disregards presumption and engenders
humility in us. Thus it becomes the gateway to the love of God for
those who bear it well. Having rejected obedience, Adam slid into
the abyss of hell;[132] the Lord, having loved it passionately, according to the salvific plan, obeyed his Father unto cross and death—
without being in any way inferior to the paternal majesty—in
order to destroy the accusation of human disobedience with his
obedience, and thus deliver all those who live in obedience into
the eternal and blessed life.[133] Anyone concerned with taking up
the struggle against the devil's presumption should concern himself with this, since obedience will show us if we advance faultlessly along all the paths of virtue.

42. Self-mastery is the name common to all the virtues. Whoever would be master of himself must exercise this self-mastery
in everything. Just as when a person suffers the loss of one of his
members—even the smallest—it deforms the entire man, even
though he retain most of his form; so too, anyone who is careless
in one virtue destroys unawares all the beauty of self-mastery. We
must not only dedicate ourselves to the corporal virtues, but also
to the ones that purify our interior. What benefit would there be
for a someone to keep his body virgin if his soul has been led into
adultery by the demon of disobedience? Or how is someone to
be rewarded for avoiding gluttony and every bodily desire, while
he never spared a thought for conceit and love of glory or was

[131] It seems that all the translations beginning with D's critical edition
identify Luke 10:27 as our author's inspiration for this text. Nonetheless,
Joest's article makes a good argument for Matt 22:37 as the proper source
since Diadochus's wording reflects Matthew's gospel and does not use the
word "strength" proper to Luke's version.
[132] Lit. *Tartarus*—as deep below Hades as earth below is below heaven.
[133] See Phil 2:6-8.

incapable of bearing a brief trial well? For all the while the scale will balance the light of justice to those who wrought works of justice in a spirit of humility.

43. It is imperative for warriors to exercise hatred of all irrational desires, to such an extent that it becomes a habit of hatred. It is necessary to maintain self-mastery with regard to food but without going so far as to disdain it, for that would be totally odious and demonic. We should not abstain from it as if it were an evil—this never! Rather, that by denying ourselves many edible delights, we keep the ardent aspect of our flesh in check and afterward that portion that remains in excess of our own needs can be distributed to beggars as a sign of sincere charity.[134]

44. Eating and drinking while giving thanks to God for what has been set before you or mixed[135] is in no way contrary to the rule of knowledge, since everything is very good.[136] But voluntarily abstaining from what is enjoyable and abundant is constitutive of knowledge and discernment. But we will not gladly forego present delights if we do not yet fully[137] taste the sweetness of God with all our sense.

45. Just as a body overburdened by the abundance of foods causes the mind to become sluggish and lazy, so too when weakened from exaggerated vigilance it brings about a certain melancholy as well as repugnance for the Word in the contemplative part of the soul. Therefore, one has to prepare foods for oneself according to the movements of the body so that when it is healthy it may be aptly kept in check. When it is weak, it should be moderately fattened. A warrior should not fatigue himself bodily but should have what he needs that he might do battle so that through bodily labors he will be sufficiently purified.

[134] See 2 Cor 8:14; 1 Tim 6:8.
[135] Drinks were often a mixed. P omits this word and R puts in its place "pour."
[136] See Gen 1:31.
[137] R translates this "with all our assurance" as does M.

46. When vanity swells up against us in a big way, if for example it should happen that some brothers or other guests arrive and you are fiercely tempted to show off, it is a good idea to permit ourselves a reasonable mitigation of our habitual regimen. Thus we dismiss the demon and reduce him to frustration and regret for his efforts. We will thus discerningly fulfill the precept of charity. And by relaxation of the rule we will keep hidden the mystery of our self-mastery.

47. Fasting, except when done before God, bears within itself its own pride. Indeed, it is like an instrument to form those who have opted for temperance. Therefore prayer-warriors should never hold themselves in high esteem but, in faith, simply keep God in view who is our goal. Indeed, even the experts at any craft never boast that their accomplishments are the result of the tools of their craft; rather, each waits for the finished project so that it might manifest the perfection of his skill.

48. Just as ground that gets the right amount of water makes the seed dropped onto it to grow in purity and abundance, so, on the contrary, the soaking of many rainstorms produces thistles and burrs. It is the same in our moderate use of wine. The soil of the heart renders pure, natural seeds and makes what the Holy Spirit has planted to yield[138] flourishingly and abundantly. But if it becomes soaked after a drinking bout, it produces thoughts of every sort—comparable to thorns and brambles.

49. When our mind floats about in the waves of excessive drink, it not only gazes passionately at the images formed by demons in its sleep, but it also fantasizes about its own comely visions for which it feverishly longs, as if in love. When the genital organs are heated by wine's warmth the mind cannot but conjure up voluptuous images. Therefore it is imperative to use wine with moderation so as to escape the dangers of excess. For then when the mind is not tricked into clinging to the sensual pleasure of

---

[138] Our author chooses a word with liturgical connotations, the same verb for "lifting up praise."

depicting sinful thoughts, it remains completely free of fantasies and, more importantly, does not become effeminate.

50. All the artificial drinks that the experts of this craft call aperitifs—doubtlessly because they open the way to the stomach for a plethora of food—should not be sought after by those who want to keep the swelling part of their bodies in check. Not only are they harmful to the health of the warriors' bodies, but also thoughtless mixing of drinks strikes a great blow to the God-bearing conscience. For what is missing from the nature of wine that its strength should be softened by mixing spices into it?

51. Our Lord Jesus Christ, master of this consecrated life, gave us an example during his passion when he was offered vinegar to drink by men under diabolical influence, in order—so it seems to me—to leave behind an example for us who are disposed to spiritual combat.[139] For it is said, those who war against sin should not have recourse to delightful foods and drinks, but rather ought perseveringly to endure the bitter struggle with patience. But let the hyssop be affixed to the ignoble sponge, so that our purification might fit the pattern more perfectly. For proper to combat is bitterness, just purification brings things to completion.[140]

52. No one can hold that going to the baths is sinful or strange. Nonetheless, abstaining from them out of a spirit of mortification is very manly and temperate. The delightful mist of the baths does not make our body effeminate, nor does it lead us to remember Adam's ignoble nudity to such a point that we should have to cover over with leaves the second reason of our own disgrace. But we above all, having barely escaped the corruption of this life, are duty-bound to unite the purity of our bodies to the beauty of moderation.

53. Nothing should hinder calling on doctors in time of illness. Indeed, given that this art is the patrimony[141] of human experience,

---

[139] P paraphrases this, "for spiritual combat."
[140] See John 19:28-29.
[141] Lit. "what is gathered together."

the remedies are already in existence.[142] Nevertheless, do not place all your hope of a cure in them but in our true Savior and Doctor Jesus Christ. This I say for the benefit of those who fruitfully exercise their self-mastery in monastic communities or in cities, yet, given their environment, cannot at all times live out their faith through love.[143] Above all, they should take care not to succumb to the devil's temptations to vainglory.[144] Nonetheless, this is why some of them brag publicly that they do not require doctors. But if someone lives the life of an anchorite in a solitary place supported by two or three brothers living the same life, let him turn in faith to the Lord alone who cures infirmities and all our weaknesses,[145] whatever affliction may befall us. For after the Lord, such a one as this has the desert as sufficient consolation in his straits. Thus such a person never is lacking in the exercise of his faith, above all because he cannot find opportunities to flaunt his virtue and patience, hidden in the desert as if behind a beautiful veil. Thus it is written, *the Lord invites the solitaries into his house.*[146]

54. When we let ourselves get excessively upset on account of bodily irregularities that can befall us, we should realize that our soul is still enslaved by the desires of the body. Thus desiring material well-being, she refuses to separate herself from the material things of this life, considering it a great loss that, on account of illness, she no longer can enjoy the springtime of youth. But if she accepts illness's afflictions with gratitude, she can be assured that she is not far from the realm of impassibility. Therefore she even joyfully accepts death since she understands this more strongly still to be the beginning of true life.

---

[142] Diadochus seems to be justifying medicines, which are a mixture of herbs, as opposed to his prohibition of mixing herbs and spices with wine. See GC 50. P, on the other hand, alters the text completely, "Providence has implanted remedies in nature."

[143] See Gal 5:6.

[144] See 1 Tim 3:6.

[145] See Matt 4: 23.

[146] Ps 67:7.

55. If the soul does not achieve a state of indifference[147] to the air it breathes, it will never desire to be separated from the body. All of the body's senses oppose faith because they only refer to present things. Faith, on the other hand, promises a treasure of future goods. It befits the warrior therefore to pay little heed to beautiful trees in bloom[148] and their comely shade, or sweet flowing brooks and ever-changing meadows, stately houses, or even growing old together with one's relatives. Nor should he, perchance, remember any flattering public honors. Rather, he thankfully makes use of what is necessary and it alone, considering this life treads a sojourner's path bereft of every carnal affection. Only by the narrow path[149] will we completely convert our thoughts toward those footsteps that lead to eternal life.

56. Our sight, our taste, and all of our senses dissipate the memory[150] of the heart when we use them immoderately, as the first Eve demonstrated for us. Indeed, she carefully remembered the divine mandate so long as she did not regard the forbidden tree with pleasure. In a certain sense she was sheltered beneath the wings of ardent love for God, thus unaware of her own nudity. But when she looked at the tree with pleasure, when she touched it with desire, and then tasted its fruit with intense pleasure, then, naked, she immediately slipped into a bodily embrace joining all her passion to it. She squandered all her desire on the joy of present things, dragging Adam along in her own fall, just for the sake of the sweet appearance of the fruit. Ever since then it has been difficult to subdue the human mind in order to remember God's commandments. Living our whole life long gazing into the depths of our hearts with undying memory of God, we ought to live as blind men throughout this deceptive life. Thus proper to a truly spiritual philosophy is to clip the wings of ardent love for visible things. This is something Job's well-experienced teaching

---

[147] Lit. "become devoid of quality."
[148] Lit. "and their fine twigs."
[149] See Matt 7:14.
[150] P adds "of God."

tells us: *if my eyes have led my heart astray.*[151] Such a rule of action is the sign of the highest self-mastery.

57. The one who dwells in the depths of his own heart escapes from this life's enchantments,[152] for walking according to the Spirit, he cannot know the desires of the flesh. Such a person walks ahead in strength of virtue, finding in those virtues the sentinels of the fortress of purity. In this way the devil's machinations against him result ineffective, even should his darts of vulgar love—so to say—penetrate the gates of his nature.

58. When our soul ceases to desire this world's enchantments, it is common that a certain tepidity[153] invades it. This hinders our ministry of the word and robs us of that acute longing for future goods. Further, it disdains this temporal life excessively, holding it as useless since it can have no good works to show for itself. It scorns knowledge itself on the grounds that it has been granted to many others as well or that it cannot promise to deliver anything perfect. We will only be able to escape passion that produces tepidity and indolence if we impose strict limits on our thoughts, returning our gaze to the memory of God alone. Only in this way will the mind succeed in returning to fervor, thus distancing itself from such an irrational dissipation.

59. When we have sealed off every venue through the memory of God, our mind will demand from us an exercise that satisfies its need for activity. Here we must let out a "Lord Jesus," as the only perfect way to achieve our goal. No one, it is said, can say *"Jesus is Lord" without the Holy Spirit.*[154] So let it [the mind] contemplate this word alone at all times in its interior treasury so as not to return to the imagination. All who ceaselessly meditate on this holy and glorious Name in the depths of their heart can see at last the light of their minds. Thus tamed by such an exacting

[151] Job 31:7.
[152] See 2 Cor 5:8.
[153] *Akēdiastēs.*
[154] 1 Cor 12:3.

effort of thought, every stain on the soul's surface is consumed in ardent feeling, for it is said, *our God is a consuming fire.*[155] Therefore the Lord invites the soul to immense love of his own glory. This is so because the mind's perseverance in the memory of that glorious and most desirable Name with an ardent heart produces in us a habitual love of his goodness. And from that moment onward, nothing can hinder it. This is the precious pearl[156] which is obtained upon having dispossessed oneself of all one's belongings and whose discovery brings about ineffable joy.

60. One thing is the joy of the beginner, quite another is that of the perfect. The first is not free from a wandering mind while the other enjoys the strength of humility. And between the two are found godly sorrow[157] and painless tears, for truly, *in much wisdom there is much knowledge and he who grows in knowledge has increase of sorrow.*[158] Therefore, it is fitting that the soul be called to its battles by this initial joy, and then be tested and proven by the truth of the Holy Spirit with regard to the evil it has done and the vain affairs it yet carries out. *You rebuke our guilt and chasten us*, as it is said; *you dissolve all we prize like a cobweb;*[159] the soul undergoes divine reproof—as if in a crucible—so that, freed of all fantasy, it might receive the power to experience joy in the fervent memory of God.

61. When the soul is agitated by anger, or blurry-eyed from a hang-over, or discouraged by onerous worries, even if it should forcefully strain itself, the mind cannot attain the memory of the Lord Jesus Christ on its own. Thus darkened by its restless passions, the mind becomes a stranger to its own sense. And so the vehemence of the passions entrenches the memory in callousness, the soul's desire finds nowhere to set its seal that the mind might bear the mark of meditation. Nevertheless, if the soul is freed of

---

[155] Deut 4:24.
[156] See Matt 13:46.
[157] See 2 Cor 7:10.
[158] Sir 1:18.
[159] Ps 38:12.

the passions, even though, through forgetfulness, the longed-for object is briefly stolen away, the mind can quickly resume its normal activity and fervently reclaim its longed-for saving treasure.

Then the soul can meditate on this grace and thereby proclaim with it, "Lord Jesus," just as a mother might teach her son to say "daddy," repeating along with him until she brings him to say it clearly—even in his sleep—and he no longer makes meaningless noises. That is why the Apostle says, *in the same way, the Spirit too comes to help us in our weakness; for we do not know how to pray as we ought, but the Spirit itself intercedes with inexpressible groans.*[160]

Given that we are child-like in our prayed utterances with regard to its perfection of virtue, we are in great need of its help so that our thoughts be penetrated and tamed by its ineffable sweetness. Thus we will be urged on to the memory and love of God our Father with all our affection. Therefore, when we are trained by [the Spirit] to call God "Father" we cry out ceaselessly in it [the Spirit], as divine Paul again says, *Abba-Father.*[161]

62. More than the other passions, ire disquiets and confuses the soul. But other times it does her a great service. Indeed, when used without agitation against the impious and every sort of libertine, whether to save or confound them, we obtain an extra dose of meekness for our souls since we necessarily converge with our goal: the justice and goodness of God. Further, by allowing ourselves to get deeply angered by sin, we often become even more virile wherever there is something of the effeminate. Nor should we doubt that though we are despondent and tremble before Death's boasting, we nonetheless show contempt before this spirit of corruption. To teach us this, our Lord's spirit was agitated and rebuked hell twice[162]—although all that he undertook, he accomplished with serenity and singularity of purpose: he returned Lazarus's soul to his body[163] and so makes me believe

---

[160] Rom 8:26.
[161] Rom 8:15.
[162] See John 12:27; 13:21.
[163] See John 11:33.

that our God and Creator did well to equip our nature with anger to be used moderately as a weapon. If only Eve would have used it against the serpent she would not have been subjected to her sensual pleasure.

Thus it seems to me that whoever is found to use measured anger with religious zeal will tip the scale of retribution in his own favor, compared with another mind which, out of sluggishness, is unmoved by anger. This second person clearly has an untrained charioteer for a mind, while the former is a warrior borne by the horses of virtue and skilled in the four-horse chariot of self-mastery and the fear of God amid devils in battle array.[164] This is the chariot of Israel about which we find written in Sacred Scripture regarding the assumption of the divine Elijah because it seems that God spoke distinctly to the Jews first about the four virtues. Precisely for that reason, that child of wisdom was wholly taken up in a chariot of fire, so it seems to me, much as the temperate person controls his personal virtue as if they were horses, when he was taken up by the spirit in the wind of fire.[165]

63. He who participates in the holy knowledge and has tasted God's sweetness should not defend himself in court nor make a motion to prosecute another—even should the clothes be taken from his back. Indeed, judges of temporal authority are in every degree inferior to the judgment of God. What is more, before divine judgment they count for nothing. Further, what difference would it make between the children of God and secular people if it was not that their justice was clearly imperfect with respect to the rights of others so that on one hand we speak of human correctness and on the other of divine righteousness?

Thus our Lord, *when he was insulted, he returned no insult; when he suffered, he did not threaten;*[166] he silently withstood[167] being stripped of his clothing, I declare, pleading to the Father for the salvation of his tormentors. But the people of this age will not

---

[164] The four horses are the cardinal virtues.
[165] See 2 Kgs 2:11.
[166] 1 Pet 2:23.
[167] P omits this.

cease with their judgments unless, at times, they recover an additional sum along with those goods for which they have entered into litigation, especially when they charge interests on a debt, to such an extent that often their judgment becomes the beginning of a great injustice.

64. I have heard from certain devout men that it is said, "we should not let the first people who come to us plunder all that we have for our own administration and for the relief of the poor—above all if we were to endure that at the hands of Christians—so we may not become partners of sin to those who harm us, for whose sake we endure mistreatment." But this is nothing other than the irrational pretext to prefer one's own property over oneself. For if I leave off praying and attending to the needs of my heart and, little by little, begin to indict those who would maltreat me and take up a place in the halls of tribunals, it is clear that I consider restituted goods over and above my salvation, not to mention the divine precept of salvation itself.

How should I follow the Gospel precept which counsels me, *if anyone wants to go to court with you over your tunic, hand him your cloak as well*,[168] if I do not, following the word of the Apostle, bear it with joy if they strip me of what I possess,[169] given that having litigated and received what he sought, the usurper is not freed of his sin. Corruptible tribunals cannot impede the incorruptible judgment of God, because these are the laws that satisfy the accused and upon which he defends his own cause. Thus it is well that we suffer the violence of those who do us evil as we pray for their repentance and not for the restitution of what they have taken from us, that they be absolved of the accusation of their deeds. That is what the justice of the Lord wants: for us to receive back, not what was lost to greed, but the greedy one freed of sin through repentance.

65. Once we have discovered the true path of piety, it is fitting and most beneficial that we sell all our belongings and distribute

---

[168] Matt 5:40.
[169] See 2 Cor 11:20.

the money according to the Lord's counsel.[170] Let us not disobey the precept of salvation with the excuse of wanting to continue to heed the commandments. In the first place, a beautiful, carefree spirit will be ours and, as a result, our poverty will be far above every sort of injustice and squabbling, since we will no longer have such possessions that ignite the fire of envy. For humility will be our warmth above all the other virtues. She [humility] will make us rest, as if naked, in her very bosom, like a mother bundling her child into her arms giving it warmth when, because of its childlike innocence, or, better, its guilelessness, it delights more in its nakedness—stripping itself, it casts its clothes somewhere far off!—than in colorful embroidered clothing. For it is written, *the Lord defends the simple, I humbled myself and he saved me.*[171]

66. The Lord will call us to accounts regarding our alms—not so much about how much we have but how much we do not have;[172] if, then, out of fear of God I hurriedly distribute just as much as I might have been able to give over a period of many years, and [as a consequence] have nothing [left], of what might I be accused? But someone might say: "Then where will their support come from in the future if the poor are accustomed to receiving something from our modest goods each day?" Such a person should learn not to insult God with his veiled avarice. God will not cease to provide for his own creature as he has always wisely done since the beginning of creation.[173] Even before this or that person felt urged to give alms, the poor still did not lack food or clothing.

To recognize how ridiculous it is to boast of our distribution of goods out of a spirit of service and hate our own desires is a beautiful thing—for that is what it means to hate one's own soul.[174] Thus, bereft of the joy of giving away money, we begin to hold

---

[170] See Matt 19:21.
[171] Ps 116:6.
[172] See 2 Cor 8:12. R misidentifies this as 2 Cor 8:18.
[173] See Matt 6:25-34.
[174] Luke 14:26.

our own soul for no account under the impression that we can do no good thing. Indeed, so long as we have abundant riches and the strength to do good we should likewise rejoice greatly in scattering them about and all the while enjoying obedience to the divine command. But when we have exhausted everything, boundless distress and humiliation enter our heart at not being able to realize more works worthy of justice. From that moment the soul turns inward in profound humility, seeking in persevering prayer, patience, and humility, what it cannot win for itself through daily almsgiving. *The poor and the indigent, it is said, will praise your name, Lord.*[175] For the gift of theology has not been prepared by God for anyone who does not prepare himself by selling all his belongings for the cause of the glory of the Gospel of God, so that in godly poverty he might proclaim the Gospel of the Kingdom of God. This is what he meant, who said, *you have prepared, O God, in your kindness, for the poor,* and added, *the Lord will give the word to those who proclaim the Gospel in much power.*[176]

67. All of God's gifts are exceedingly beautiful[177] and attain every benefit, but none of them moves and makes our[178] heart to burn with love for his goodness as much as *theologia.* Being an early offshoot of God's grace, it grants the soul those gifts which are doubtlessly the most important of all.[179] In the first place, it prepare us joyfully to disdain every affection for this life, given that instead of corruptible desires, we possess the ineffable riches of God's words. It illumines our intellect in the fire of transformation and then brings it to enter into communion with those spirits that serve the Lord.[180] Those of us, beloved, who have already been truly prepared for it desire this beautiful virtue, a thoroughly

---

[175] Ps 74:21.
[176] Ps 67:11-12.
[177] P translates this as "flawless."
[178] R omits this word.
[179] R adds ""freely and completely."
[180] See Heb 1:14.

contemplative friend,[181] which achieves freedom from every worry, which, in the brilliance of indescribable light, nourishes the mind on the words of God. In a word, through the holy prophets the rational mind is united with the divine Logos in an indissoluble communion, so that even among human beings—O wonder!— this godly bridesmaid[182] might harmonize the divinized voices which sing clearly of God's magnificence.

68. Often our mind finds it difficult to bear the many things prayer holds since it is very taxing and because of the subtlety of this virtue so desired. But *theologia* gives of itself joyfully and divine contemplation frees up [the mind] making it open and expansive. So as not to fall into the desire of speaking much, and to prevent the mind from immoderate exaltation[183] in its joy, we should spend the greatest amount of time possible in prayer, the Psalms, reading of Sacred Scripture, and be sure not to neglect the considerations of the learned, whose faith is made manifest in their words. Acting this way will preserve our mind from mixing its own language with the language of grace. This will also preserve us from excessive joy and the vain multiplication of words. Rather, during our prayer times we will protect our mind from imagination and will assure that most of our thoughts end in tears.

[181] *Proxenos*, a public guest or host representing a nation. Diadochus seems to make this virtue God's ambassador. Perhaps given the difficult relation of concepts, A, D, M, P, R, and T omit it while F translates it as *Gastgäberin* ("host").

[182] *Nymphaphōgos*: the chaperone who guides the bride to the house of the groom and ultimately to his chamber (See Ps 45:14, The Royal Wedding Song, which says, "Dressed on brocades, the king's daughter is led to the king, with bridesmaids in her train"). *Theologia* is this mediation that leads the soul to union with God and introduces us to his nuptial mysteries. For Diadochus, *theologia* is always mystical. A omits translating this word, D translates it as *initiatrice divine*, M does not attempt to translate it but leaves it in Greek, P paraphrases it with "like one who conducts the wedding feast," while R ("bridesmaid") and F (*göttliche Brautführerin*) concur. In GC 79 Diadochus quotes this psalm directly with regard to the soul as an intimate place where God and the human bride are alone together, outside of the enemy's reach.

[183] Lit. "immoderately taking to flight."

Resting in times of stillness and especially when penetrated by the sweetness of prayer not only helps to overcome those aforementioned faults, but more and more it brings about a renewal of divine contemplation, permitting us to advance quickly with much humility in discernment of God's light. Further, one should be aware that there is a prayer beyond all expansion. But this is given only to those fully awake and filled with God's grace.

69. At first it is normal for grace to illumine the soul, with great feeling, with its own light. But as combat continues, it proceeds to work its mysteries unobserved in the soul of the theologian, in order to later incite us to follow his footprints rejoicing in divine contemplation, as people called from ignorance to knowledge.[184] Even as it does this, amid many struggles, it guards our knowledge from conceit. On the one hand we should be somewhat saddened feeling ourselves as people abandoned so that we humble ourselves more and better submit ourselves to the glory of God. On the other hand, we should know when to rejoice when lifted by the wings of good hope. As excessive sadness encompasses the soul with despair and faithlessness, so too excessive joy arouses presumption. Of course, I am referring to those who are still infants,[185] because between illumination and abandonment stands the experience of trial—just as hope stands between despair and presumption. It is written, *I waited patiently for the Lord; he bent down and heard my cry;*[186] and further, *according to numerous sufferings of my heart, your blessings have gladdened my heart.*[187]

70. As when the doors of the baths are left open it causes the heat to escape from inside, so too, when a soul wants to speak much, even though all that he has to say is good, she dissipates the memory through the door of the voice. Thus deprived of opportune thoughts a soul unloads her indiscreet considerations on

---

[184] R translates this as "from lack of perception to perception."
[185] See 1 Cor 13:11; Eph 4:14; 1 Thess 2:7; Heb 5:12f.
[186] Ps 40:2.
[187] Ps 94:19.

the first person she runs in to, because she no longer has the Holy Spirit who protects her thoughts from fantasy. For the good always shuns verbosity since it is at odds with every sort of disorder and fantasy. Therefore opportune silence is good and nothing else is the mother of the wisest thoughts.

71. The word of knowledge itself teaches us that the novice soul given over to theology is easily disturbed by a host of passions, above all ire and hatred. She suffers this more on account of her own personal spiritual progress than on account of a great number of demons stirring up the passions. Thus, so long as the soul is inclined toward worldly-mindedness, she is capable of standing idly by and unmoved watching justice trampled underfoot by others. This is so because she is more concerned with her own cares and such a soul does not look to God. But when she begins to transcend her own passions through the love for God and the scorn for present things, she cannot bear to see justice violated even in her dreams and is stirred to anger toward the evildoers. Such a one is in turmoil until she sees those who harm justice are obliged to ask pardon with pious words. On one hand the soul hates the unjust, but on the other hand, she has a preferential love for the just.[188] The eye of the soul will escape every distraction when her veil—by that I mean the body—is woven into something ethereal[189] by way of self-mastery. Nonetheless,

---

[188] See Heb 1:9; Ps 44:8.

[189] This particularly difficult passage finds little consent among translators. *Leptotēta pollēn . . . exuphēnē.* The concepts have to do with something very thin (*leptotēta pollēn*) and something woven or perfected. Thus A translates this as *se vuelve un tejido muy delgado* ("turns into a very thin cloth"); D translates the phrase as *reduit a un tres fin tissue* ("reduced to a very fine cloth or tissue"?); F says *zu ganz besondere Dichte gewoben ist* ("woven into a very special material"); M has the following: *ridotta a sottilissimsa trama* ("reduced to a most subtle fabric"); P makes it "is refined to near-transparency"; R seems to contradict the sense of *exuphene*, which suggests perfection or something completed, with her rendition: "unravels into a great thinness." T chose to translate this as *ad multam tenuitem . . . redegit* ("reduced to great lightness"). Given Diadochus's dualistic tendencies I opted for my translation to reflect the sense of angelism that underlies Diadochus's anthropology.

better than hating the unjust is to weep for their insensitivity, because even if they are worthy of hatred, the Word does not want the God-friendly soul to be disquieted by hatred because knowledge does not work in a soul where there is hatred.

72. The theologian who is satisfied and set aflame by the very words of God, sets his soul, after many vicissitudes,[190] onto the wide open path of impassibility. For it is written, *the words of God are chaste, silver tested in fire and purified of every stain.*[191] The gnostic, in his turn, fortified by his experience, rises above passions. The theologian, if he remains humble, tastes the gnostic's experience. The gnostic, if he learns his part of infallible discernment of spirits, acquires a little contemplative virtue. The two gifts do not concur entirely in the same person so that through their awareness of what each other has excelled in, they might overflow with humility even as they are filled with the zeal of righteousness, as the Apostle says, *to one is given through the Spirit the expression of wisdom; to another the expression of knowledge according to the same Spirit.*[192]

73. When the soul enjoys the fullness of its innate fruits, she sings the Psalms with more strength and prefers to pray with a louder voice. But when she is moved by the Holy Spirit, she chants and prays in the solitude of her own heart with all abandon and sweetness. The former disposition is accompanied by joy, thus awakening the imagination; the latter, on the other hand, by spiritual tears followed by a longing for silence. For the memory keeps its warmth when the voice is moderated and it prepares the heart to express itself with tearful and joyous thoughts. In this way the seeds of contemplation sown in tears are made manifest in the soil of the heart because of the joyful hope of its harvest.[193]

When we are burdened by heavy discouragement we should raise our voices a bit more in psalmody, making the sounds of the

---

[190] F, M, P, R, and T omit this for some reason.
[191] Ps 11:7.
[192] 1 Cor 12:8.
[193] See Ps 125:5-6.

soul harmonize with hope's joy unto such point that the dark clouds are driven away by the breath of song.

74. When a soul has arrived at self-knowledge she engenders a fervor pleasing to God. Because she is not shaken by life's worries she produces a desire for peace that seeks God who in turn grants a similar peace. But she is quickly distracted from her memory and betrayed by her senses because nature too soon squanders its own poor resources as a result of its idleness. That is why the wise men of Greece did not achieve what they sought through self-mastery, because their minds were not moved by eternal and ever-true Wisdom. But the fervor granted to the heart by the Holy Spirit is, in the first place, peaceful and unyielding. It arouses every part of the soul to long for God, not blown about outside one's heart but all through it delighting the entire person in charity and boundless joy.[194] Now, one has to identify the first[195] in order to possess the second; for on the one hand natural love is a sign of a certain natural health through self-master, but on the other it [self-mastery] can never benefit the mind in favor of impassibility as spiritual love can.

75. Just as this air around us is kept pure by the north wind that blows across creation,[196] because this wind is subtle and clear by nature, and the south wind makes the entire atmosphere dense and by its nature produces fog which, as related to clouds, are brought together to cover all the earth, so too, when the soul is moved by the breath of the Holy Spirit of truth, she is found [to be] free of diabolical fog; but when she is blown on violently by the spirit of deceit she is totally covered by clouds of sin. Therefore, we need to use all of our strength to orient our purpose toward the life-giving and purifying breeze of the Holy Spirit— that is, toward that wind which the prophet Ezekiel saw, by the light of knowledge, coming from the north,[197] so that, above all,

---

[194] P and R add "*through* the heart."
[195] Both P and R insert the word "ardor" here.
[196] F fails to translate "across creation" for some reason.
[197] See Ezek 1:4.

the contemplative element of our spirit remains clear. Thus will we be able to abandon ourselves to divine contemplation without danger of error, seeing the splendor of this light that is the light of true knowing.[198]

76. Some have maintained that grace and sin, that is, the Spirit of Truth and the spirit of deceit, are both hidden in the intellect of the baptized. Consequently, so it is said, one of them induces the mind of a person to good and the other immediately afterward induces the mind to the opposite. But from Sacred Scripture and my own sense of reason I have concluded that before holy baptism grace admonishes the mind from without, while Satan lurks in the depths of the mind, trying to seal off all available exits of the mind. But in the moment in which we are regenerated the demon is expelled to the exterior and grace is within. So we find that just as deceit reigned in the soul before, so too after baptism truth reigns. Nonetheless, Satan continues working on the soul as before and often even more strongly. This is not to say he is present concurrently with grace—never!—rather, he clouds the intellect through the body's softness and the sweetness of irrational pleasures. And this occurs because God lets it happen, so that, passing through tempests and trials by fire, one might, if he so desires, come to enjoy the good.[199] For it is said, *we passed through fire and water; then you led us out to relief.*[200]

77. From the moment of baptism, as I mentioned, grace hides itself in the depths of the mind, its presence concealed even from our very senses. But when one begins to long for God with total conviction, then in sublime colloquy [grace] communicates a portion of its wealth to the soul through the intellect's senses.

From the moment in which he has firmly set his heart upon complete possession of what he has discovered his desire is such that he is happily willing to abandon all of this world's present

---

[198] R translates this as "true perception."
[199] P makes this word "divine blessings."
[200] Ps 66:12.

goods in order truly to acquire the field in which the treasure of this life lies hidden.[201]

When you have renounced ownership of every kind of wealth in this life you then discover the place where the grace of God lies hidden. Further, according to the soul's progress the divine gift reveals its goodness to the mind. Nonetheless, even in this case, the Lord permits the soul to be burdened by demons in order to teach her the value of discernment of good and evil, and to render her humbler still, because the discomfiting diabolical thoughts shame the soul even as it is purified.

78. It is in the soul with its intellectual movement that we are in the image of God, and the body is akin to its dwelling place. Therefore, Adam's transgression not only caused the lineaments of the soul's form to be marred, but the body too fell into corruption. Thus it was for the soul and the body that the holy Word of God was made flesh and, as God, liberally grants us the water of salvation through the baptism of regeneration. Through the action of the life-giving and Holy Spirit we are regenerated. Thus we are purified immediately in body and soul—that is, if one is completely oriented toward God—because the Holy Spirit takes up residence[202] in us and sin is evicted from us. So it is impossible that in the soul's simple and integral form two persons could subsist—as some hold. Since through the baptismal bath divine grace adheres to the lineaments of the image—as a guarantee of likeness—where is the Evil One[203] going to stay, for what partnership do light and darkness have with one another?[204] We who have taken up the course of holy combat[205] believe that through the bath of incorruptibility the multiform serpent is cast out of the treasure chamber of the intellect. Nor should we be surprised if after our baptism, along with good things, we should also think

---

[201] See Matt 13:44.
[202] Lit. "to pitch one's camp."
[203] Lit. "person of the evil one."
[204] 2 Cor 6:14.
[205] See Heb 12:1.

crude things. For the bath of sanctity takes away[206] from us the stain of sin, but it does not change this two-way inclination of our desire, nor does it impede demons from making war against us or speaking deceitful words to us, so that what, as carnal people,[207] we are incapable of protecting, we do indeed preserve through the power of God insofar as we take up the weapons of righteousness.

79. Satan, as I have said, is cast out of the soul through holy Baptism; but for reasons mentioned above, he is permitted to act on her through the body. In fact, the grace of God dwells in the depths of the soul, that is, in the mind, for it is written, *the glory of the king's daughter*, as it says, *is interior*,[208] and is thus invisible to demons.[209] That is why we perceive, from the depths of our hearts, a longing for God which wells up whenever we fervently remember God. Consequently, evil spirits assault our bodily senses and then hide behind carnal inclinations[210] working in those who are still "children" in the soul. Therefore, the Apostle says, *our spirit takes great delight in the laws of the spirit*,[211] while our senses let themselves be dragged about by easy pleasure. As a result, grace, by way of the spiritual sense, makes the body rejoice with ineffable exultation in those who advance in knowledge.[212] But the demons violently take the soul prisoner by way of the

---

[206] Lit. "to take away from all around."

[207] See 1 Cor 2:14-15, Paul's use of the term *psychikos* ("carnal man") as opposed to *pneumatikos* ("spiritual person"). R's translation—"this is so that in taking up the weapons of justice, we might keep, in the power of God, that which we have not preserved through having souls"—seems to miss this reference.

[208] Ps 45:14.

[209] Centuries later Saint John of the Cross would say the same thing in his *Dark Night of the Soul*, 2.23.1: "since the soul walked in darkness in the way we mentioned, she was concealed and hidden from the devil, and from his deceits and wiles." See also book 2.24.3; and *Letter* 8.

[210] See Matt 26:41.

[211] See Rom 7:22.

[212] John of the Cross says that graces received produce joy in the spirit but can even have erotic effects in the spiritually immature.

bodily senses, especially when they find us negligent in running the race of piety, inciting her—murderers that they are—to do what she does not want to do.

80. Those who maintain that within the heart of the believer grace and sin are equally present as two different persons base their argument on what the Evangelist says, *the light shines in the darkness, and the darkness has not overcome it.*[213] They want to back up their position holding that the divine splendor is in no way sullied cohabiting with evil regardless, they say, of how closely in the soul the divine light draws near to the demonic darkness.[214] Just a word from the Gospel should convince them that their thought is foreign to Sacred Scripture. Indeed, given that the Word of God, true light, deigned to appear in the flesh to his own creation, through his infinite kindness to humankind he lit in us the light of his holy knowledge. But the spirit of the world does not understand God's design, that is, it does not recognize it, *for the concern of the flesh is hostility toward God.*[215] The Theologian[216] uses similar words. After a few more words the Divine adds, *the true light, which enlightens everyone, was coming into the world*, meaning he guides and gives life; *he was in the world, and the world came to be through him, but the world did not know him. He came to what was his own, but his own people did not receive*[217] *him. But to those who did accept him he gave power to become children of God, to those who believe in his name.*[218] And wisest Paul says the same thing when interpreting "not receiving."[219] *It is not that I have already taken hold*[220] *of it or have already attained perfect maturity, but I continue my pursuit in*

---

[213] John 1:5.

[214] See 2 Cor 6:14.

[215] Rom 8:7.

[216] Saint John the Evangelist.

[217] *Parelabon* ("receive, seize, take possession of"). Diadochus will use a derivation of this word with *katalambanō* when quoting Saint Paul a few lines later.

[218] John 1:9-12.

[219] *Katelaben*.

[220] *Elabon*.

hope that I may possess[221] *it, since I have indeed been taken possession*[222] *of by Christ Jesus.*[223] So, according to the Evangelist, it is not Satan who has not accepted the true light, since he was estranged from it from the beginning, since it does not shine in him. On the contrary, he refers to people who, having heard of the powerful works and wonders of the Son of God, did not want to approach the light of the knowledge of him on account of their darkened hearts.[224] It is for this reason that he fittingly rebuffs them.

81. The word of knowledge teaches us that there are two species of evil spirits: some are more subtle while others are more material. The more subtle ones fight against the soul, while the others hold the flesh captive[225] by means of lecherous provocation. Therefore the demons who fight against the soul and the demons who fight against the body oppose each other, even when they are both resolved to bring about harm to people. When grace does not dwell in a person, they conceal themselves like serpents in the depths of the heart, prohibiting that the soul fix its gaze on the desire of the good. But when grace has hidden itself in the mind, then they penetrate[226] parts of the heart like gloomy clouds, taking the shape of the passions of sin and varied forms of dissipation, in order to cloud the mind's memory and strip it of its rapport with grace. And so, when the passions of the soul are afire in us by the demons who bother the soul and, above all, by presumption, which is the mother of all vices, then it is that thinking about the dissolution of our body we shame puffed up vanity. We have to do the same thing when the demons who wrestle with the body set the heart to boil in its shameful desires, because just this mere consideration of the memory of God is enough to render every type of evil spirit ineffective. If, on the other hand, the demons attacking our souls suggest, based on this consideration, an un-

---

[221] *Katelabo.*
[222] *Katelephthen.*
[223] Phil 3:12.
[224] See Rom 1:20-21; 11:10; Eph 4:18.
[225] Lit. "to take prisoner of war."
[226] Lit. "run through."

limited contempt for our human nature as if the flesh were worthless (something they love to do when they want to torture us through thoughts),[227] then let us consider the honor and the glory of the Kingdom of Heaven, without losing from view the bitter somberness of judgment, in order that our discouragement be consoled by one, and our facile-spirited heart be reprimanded by the other.

82. The Lord teaches us in the Gospels[228] that when Satan returns and finds the house swept and desolate, that is, a sterile heart, he then gathers seven other demons, enters the heart, hides there and makes this last state of the person worse than before. Therefore, we have to think that when the Holy Spirit is within us Satan cannot enter or remain in the depths of a soul.[229] Divine Paul clearly teaches us the meaning of this contemplation by way of the example of spiritual combat: *For I take delight in the law of God in my inner self, but I see in my members another principle at war with the law of my mind, making me captive to the law of sin that dwells in my members;*[230] and of perfection he says further, *hence, now there is no condemnation for those who are in Christ Jesus. For the law of the spirit of life in Christ freed me from the law of sin and death.*[231] Elsewhere, to teach us that Satan fights with the body against the soul that participates in the Holy Spirit, he says, *so stand fast with your loins girded in truth, arrayed in righteousness for a breastplate, and your feet shod in readiness for the gospel of peace. In every circumstance, take faith as a shield, to quench all [the] flaming arrows of the evil one. And take the helmet of salvation and the sword of the Spirit, which is the word of God.*[232] One thing is captivity and quite another is combat, because the former means violent capture, while the latter points to a struggle between equal powers. Therefore, the Apostle says that the devil attacks Christ-bearing souls with fiery darts,

---

[227] See Luke 8:28.
[228] See Matt 12:44-45.
[229] See GC 78.
[230] Rom 7:22-23.
[231] Rom 8:1-2.
[232] Eph 6:14-17.

because he who does not dominate his adversary always uses arrows against him in order to take prisoner the one fighting against him from a distance with arrows. Thus Satan, given that he cannot hide from those whose soul is in grace, as he did previously, resorts to altering the warrior's emotions,[233] flying at the body and hiding in it, and through its attractions he attempts to rope in the soul.[234]

Therefore, it is necessary discreetly to let the body waste away so that the spirit does not give in to its emotions and slide into the ease of pleasure. For this reason it is fitting that we hold firm to the apostolic dictum that says that the warriors under the action of divine light *delight in the law of the Lord,*[235] *becoming its slave.*[236] But the flesh is too pliable and through its facile attractions it gives into the evil spirits. Thus it is dragged into the service of evil. Here it is clearly manifest that the mind is not the common dwelling place of God and the devil; *because, how do I myself, with my mind, serve the law of God but, with my flesh, the law of sin,*[237] if my mind is not rooted in total freedom in order to fight against demons, serving joyfully the goodness of grace, while the body freely welcomes the perfumes of irrational pleasures? As I said, it is permitted of evil spirits of deceit to hide themselves in the bodies of warriors who resist sin amid combat—for the apostle says, *for I know that good does not dwell in me, that is, within my flesh.*[238] The Apostle does not say this of himself: demons fight against the intellect, but through the ease of pleasures [gradually brought on by] lascivious consolations they try to debilitate the flesh. According to a reasonable opinion, they are permitted to dwell in the depths of the body, even of those who fight incessantly against sin, because the independent human spirit is always put to the test. But if a living person undergoes death through his efforts,

---

[233] Lit. "softness."
[234] See Matt 26:41.
[235] Rom 7:22.
[236] Rom 14:18; 1 Cor 9:27.
[237] Rom 7:25.
[238] Rom 7:18.

he would then become wholly the house of the Holy Spirit, because such a one has risen even before he dies, just as the blessed Paul did, as do all who flawlessly fought and do fight against sin.

83. It is the heart which produces thoughts, both good and not good. But it is not that it produces such evil thoughts by nature. Rather, it is through the original deceit that it once and for all has as a habit the memory of evil.[239] Nonetheless, it conceives the greater portion of evil thoughts on account of the demons' bitterness. However, we feel as if they all came from our own heart, and therefore some held that sin coexists in the mind along with grace. That is why they relate what the Lord said, *but everything that comes out of the mouth comes from the heart, and that is what defiles man. For from the heart come evil thoughts, adultery,* and so forth.[240] They do not know that our mind, possessing the subtle faculty of the sense, makes its own the action of the thoughts suggested to it by evil spirits, by way of the flesh as it were. By way of complicity, the body's malleability draws it more toward the soul in a way unknown to us.[241] The flesh always loves to be adulated without measure by such trickery, so it seems that the thoughts sown by demons originate in the heart. On the other hand, we actually do appropriate them when we desire to be gratified by them. This is what the Lord reproached, just as the divine aphorism reveals to us when he used the expression cited above. Since one who finds pleasure in the thoughts suggested by Satan's malice and imprints their memory on his heart, it is clear that from that moment onward he bears the fruit of his own reflections

84. The Lord says in the Gospels[242] that the strong man cannot be expelled from his abode unless the one who is stronger chains him, strips him, and casts him out. How can one who has been so shamefully expelled, even if he were to want to, enter once

---

[239] Note the juxtaposition of memory of God/memory of evil.
[240] Matt 15:18-19.
[241] See Matt 26:41.
[242] See Matt 12:49.

again and continually reside with the true lord who rests in his own dwelling? A king, in fact, having deposed a tyrant who opposes him does not dream of admitting him to share his royal courts; rather he cuts him down immediately or, at least, he delivers him over to his own soldiers to be bound up for a drawn-out torture and a miserable death.

85. If one were to think that because we have both good and evil thoughts both the Holy Spirit and the devil dwell together in the intellect,[243] let him understand that this occurs because we have neither tasted nor seen how good the Lord is.[244] In the first place, to be sure, and as I have said above,[245] grace hides its presence in the baptized, awaiting the soul's movement. When the entire person turns toward the Lord, then she [grace], in an ineffable movement, manifests her presence in the heart and awaits once again the soul's movement, permitting that the devil's darts penetrate unperceived unto the most intimate sense, so that in an even more fervent resolve and humble disposition, the soul seeks God. For the rest, if the person begins to advance in the observance of the commandments and continuously invokes the Lord, then the fire of holy grace spreads even to the external senses of his heart, burning the chaff of the human soil completely. Thus, even the demonic darts land far from these parts and only lightly pierce the passionate part of the soul. Finally, when the combatant has dressed[246] himself in all the virtues and, above all, perfect poverty, then grace illumines all of his nature with an ever deeper sentiment, setting it ablaze with great love for God. From that moment onward, the demonic bowshots are extinguished outside of the body's senses. Thus the breeze of the Holy Spirit which moves the heart toward those winds of peace extinguishes even those demon-borne fiery darts in midair.[247] Further, one who has

---

[243] See GC 78.
[244] See Ps 34:9.
[245] See GC 77.
[246] Lit. "to bind around oneself."
[247] See Eph 6:16.

advanced to this degree God sometimes abandons to the devil's wickedness and the darkening of the intellect so that our freedom not be completely chained up by the bonds of grace—not only so that sin is defeated by his fight, but also because the person should continue to proceed into the spiritual trial. For whatever the disciple considers perfect in himself is actually an imperfection with respect to God's ambition which instructs us with a love that seeks to surpass his own achievements, climbing to the top[248] of the ladder that appeared to Jacob.

86. The Lord himself says that Satan, like a lightning bolt, fell from Heaven,[249] to prevent this perverted being from peering into the dwelling place of the holy angels. How then could he, who is not considered worthy of communion with the good servants, share God's dwelling place in the human mind?[250] They will say—without saying more—that this happens in relation to desolation. Indeed, corrective desolation does not deprive the soul of divine light in any way whatsoever. As I have already said,[251] frequently grace merely hides its presence within the soul, so that impelled by the devil's bitterness, the soul progresses through seeking God's assistance with all fear and great humility, thus recognizing little by little the evil deeds of the enemy. [God] is like a mother who momentarily refuses to carry in her arms her little one who is unruly[252] with regard to nursing so that, thus frightened by the foul-looking men and the beasts that surround him, he goes back to his mother's lap in tears and great fear. But the desolation produced from turning away [from God] leaves the soul unwilling to possess God a prisoner to the demons, as it were. But we are not children of desertion[253]—far from it!—but we believe ourselves to be legitimate children of God's grace, and we are nursed by it through little desolations and rich consolations, so that, in his

---

[248] Lit. "completely scale."
[249] See Luke 10:18.
[250] Once again our author launches an argument against the Messalians.
[251] See GC 77 and 85.
[252] Lit. "not docile to the rules of nursing."
[253] See Heb 10:39.

goodness, we might urge ourselves on to become perfect in the fullness of maturity.[254]

87. [God's] pedagogical desolation brings about in the soul profound sorrow, humiliation, and a degree of despair, so that the glory-seeking and timorous parts be led to humility, as is fitting. Quickly it brings fear of God and tears of confession upon the heart and a deep desire for beautiful silence.[255] That desolation which occurs on account of infidelity to God leaves the soul filled with despair mixed with faithlessness, pride, and anger. Understanding the experience of both types of desolation we must then go to God with the dispositions proper to each. In the first case we ought to offer him thanksgiving along with contrition as the one disciplining our undisciplined mind in the school of consolation, as a good father teaching the difference between virtue and vice. In the second case we should offer Him unceasing confession of our sins, tears without end, and greater solitude, so that by way of added effort we can petition God to look upon our heart as he did before. But one ought to know that when the battle between Satan and the soul takes the form of a confrontation—here I am referring to the pedagogical desolation—grace, as I said before,[256] hides itself but operates invisibly aiding the soul in order to show its enemies that victory belongs to the soul alone.

88. When someone in the winter season stands out in the open facing East at the break of day, the front of his body is warmed by the sun, but his back is deprived of all warmth because the sun is not yet over his head. That is how it is for those who are just beginning spiritual activity. They have their hearts only partially warmed by holy grace. Thus their mind can begin its fruitful spiritual thought, but the visible parts of the heart continue thinking according to the flesh, since not all their members are illumined in the depth of their sense by the light of holy grace. And not understanding this, some have thought that there are two opposing

---

[254] See Eph 4:13.
[255] Notice the relation between silence and tears as seen in GC 73.
[256] GC 86.

forces contending with each other within the minds of warriors. And so it happens that the soul thinks good and evil things at the same time, just as that person in our example who shivers and feels warm at the same time when he is touched by the warmth of the sun. And so, from the moment in which our mind has slid into this double knowledge, it then produces good and bad thoughts at the same time, even though it does not choose to do so—and this above all in those who have come to experience the subtleties of discernment. Even as the mind strives to think of good things, soon it remembers evil things, given that ever since Adam's disobedience human memory is divided in double thought. If we begin then, to fulfill God's commandments with fervent zeal, from that moment onward grace will illumine all of our senses with deep sentiments, as if it were burning our thoughts and penetrating our heart with the peace of unyielding friendship, preparing us to consider things spiritually rather than carnally. This is what frequently occurs to those who approach perfection—to those who ceaselessly keep within their hearts the memory of the Lord Jesus.[257]

89. Through the regeneration of baptism holy grace obtains two benefits for us, one of which infinitely surpasses the other. It grants us the first immediately, since we are renewed in the water itself which washes us of every stain of sin and it restores all the etchings of the soul—that is, making evident what is "the image"[258]—cleansing it of every stain of sin.[259] The other part, which is "the likeness," he hopes to bring about with our cooperation. When the mind begins to taste the goodness of the Holy Spirit with profound sentiments, then we ought to know that grace is beginning to paint the likeness over the image. In the

---

[257] This is the path to perfection for Diadochus.

[258] See Gen 1:27. Diadochus uses the image of God as the original icon painter who begins his work first with an etching (image) and finishes with paint (likeness), obliquely referring to Saint Paul's phrase, "we are God's work of art" (Eph 2:9). In *Hom.* 30, 4 (242) Macarius-Symeon makes Christ the Painter as does Gregory of Nyssa in his *Commentary on the Song of Songs*, 15.

[259] See Eph 5:27. See GC 78.

same way, in fact, that painters first sketch the figure of a person in one color, and then little by little make it flourish with one pigmentation upon another, reflecting even the model's hair faithfully, so too the grace of God first establishes a sketch of "in the image" through baptism as when the human was first created. When grace sees that we desire with all our heart the beauty of the likeness and to be naked and without fear[260] in its workshop, then it makes virtue flourish upon virtue;[261] thus elevating the soul's beauty from glory to glory,[262] it places upon it the distinguishing marks of "the likeness." In this way the spiritual sense reveals that we have been formed "in the likeness," yet it is through illumination that we will know the perfection of likeness. The mind receives all the other virtues through sense, proportionately advancing with ineffable rhythm; but no one can attain spiritual love if he is not illumined in all certainty by the Holy Spirit. Since the mind does not perfectly receive "the likeness" by divine light, even though little by little it attained nearly all the other virtues, it would still remain deprived of perfect love. Indeed, when it has been made alike to God's virtue—I mean, according to the measure in which a person accepts to be made similar to God—he then bears the likeness of divine love.[263] Just as in all portraits the flourishing details of colors added to the image retain the likeness of the model—even in his smile—so too in those who have been painted "in the likeness" by divine grace. When love's illumination is applied to "the image," it is clear that "the likeness" is wholly beautiful. No other virtue attains impassibility for the soul save love alone, *because love is the fullness of the law*.[264] As our inner man is renewed in the taste of love day by day,[265] so is its perfection accomplished.

---

[260] See Gen 2:25 "naked and without shame."

[261] See John 1:16.

[262] See 2 Cor 3:18.

[263] Diadochus uses a Platonic form, alluding to *The Republic*, 501b, 613a7-bl.

[264] Rom 13:10.

[265] See 2 Cor 4:16.

90. If we fervently long for God's virtue, at the outset of our progress the Holy Spirit lets the soul taste God's sweetness in a total sense of fullness, so that the mind might have keen awareness of the ultimate prize for efforts which so please God. But later it will often hide the richness of this life-giving gift so that, even though we should attain all the other virtues, we will consider ourselves as nothing if we do not yet have the habit of holy love. This is when the devil of hatred increases his attacks on the souls of the warriors in such a way that they accuse of hatred even those who love them, and their kiss conceals mortal hatred.[266] From that moment onward, the soul suffers much more. On the one hand, it retains the memory of spiritual love, yet on the other hand, it cannot attain it in the spiritual sense for lack of those trials that bring about complete perfection. Therefore it is necessary to abnegate oneself in order to arrive at its taste with all one's sense and complete certainty. This is so because no one still in the flesh can attain his perfection except the saints who make it to martyrdom and perfect confession. Therefore, he who has attained this is completely transformed and would not wantonly grasp for food,[267] for what desire for the goods of this world could there be for one who is nourished on divine love? Therefore, wisest Paul— that great deposit of knowledge—who proclaimed to us the fullness of the future delights of the first among the just, says the following: *For the kingdom of God is not food and drink, but righteousness, peace, and joy in the Holy Spirit.*[268] All of that is the fruit of perfect charity. And so, those who progress toward perfection can continually taste it from here below, but no one can attain perfection, except when the mortal part is swallowed up by life.[269]

91. Someone from among those who love the Lord with unyielding resolve once told me the following:[270] "Because I longed

---

[266] Lit. "bears ruinous acts of hatred."

[267] See Gen 3:6, the original fall through grasping at forbidden food, and Phil 2:6, the New Adam who did not grasp at being Divine.

[268] Rom 14:17.

[269] See 2 Cor 5:4; 1 Cor 15:54, which cites Isa 25:8.

[270] Our author is actually referring to himself, as in GC 13.

for conscious knowledge of the love of God, he who is Goodness itself granted it to me; and ever since I have experienced the action of this sense with full certainty to such a degree that my soul was spurred on with joyful desire and ineffable love so that it quit my body to go with the Lord[271]—to the point of almost losing all awareness of this passing life."

Therefore, one who has arrived at the experience of this love, even though he is hurt by a myriad insults from someone, he endures as if he were united to the soul of the one who insults and wounds him.[272] He only becomes incensed with those who go against the poor or God, as the Scriptures say,[273] "speakers of iniquity," or those who live in some other evil way. He who from now on loves God more than himself—or better still, who does not love himself at all, but God alone—no longer defends his own honor, rather his sole desire is that the justice of God[274] who has bestowed upon him eternal honor be praised. This he does not desire half-heartedly,[275] but rather he has this habitual attitude resultant of the great experience he has had of divine love.

On the other hand, one ought to know that in the moment in which someone is spurred on by God to such a degree of love, he is elevated beyond faith because when he reaches the very peaks of love; he now possesses him in the keen sense of his heart whom he first honored with faith. The holy Apostle clearly preaches to us when he says, *So faith, hope, love remain, these three; but the greatest of these is love.*[276] In fact, he who possesses God through the abundance of love, as I already mentioned, is much greater than his own faith, for he is immersed[277] in desire.

---

[271] See 2 Cor 12:2.

[272] His malefactor.

[273] See Ps 74: 6.

[274] The text says "him," but in order to avoid confusion I have inserted the Divine Name.

[275] Lit. "with little will."

[276] 1 Cor 13:13.

[277] Lit. "he is wholly in longing."

92. In the middle stage of the operations of divine knowledge we undergo grief to no small degree if, on account of some irritation, we have offended someone thus making him our enemy. Therefore it does not cease to prick our conscience until with great contrition we bring the offended person back to his original disposition. But its worst sting is when a worldly person becomes unjustly angry with us. It leads us to much talk and exaggerated consideration[278] about it, and we become a scandal for those who lead worldly lives.[279] As a result the mind becomes lazy as far as contemplation is concerned since the word of knowledge which is made up completely of love does not allow the mind to open itself to understand the divine lessons upon which it meditates, unless we have first taken back in love the one who is groundlessly set against us. But if he does not want it to come to that or avoids the places we frequent, then knowledge impels us to keep the precept of love in the intimacy of our heart, making the image of his face the object of our good dispositions and affections. Indeed, it is said that if anyone desires the knowledge of God, he ought to consider without anger the face of even those who are angry with him for no reason at all. Fulfilling this, not only is the mind flawlessly moved by *theologia*, but it ascends with great boldness to the love of God, as if urged on unhindered from the second stage to the first.

93. To those who begin to long for piety, the path of virtue seems harsh and depressing—not because it is, but because human nature lives among vast pleasures from the moment of leaving the womb. But for those who are capable of walking beyond the half-way point, it seems an even and easy path. In fact, submitted to good habits through the exercise of the good, the bad expires along with the memory of those irrational pleasures.[280] From that moment onward, the soul takes to the well-worn path of virtue with joy. That is why the Lord upon introducing us to the road of

---

[278] Lit. "over concerned consideration."
[279] Lit. "speak from this age." See Rom 14:33; 1 Cor 2:6.
[280] One bad habit can only be overcome through forming a good habit.

salvation, says: *How narrow the gate and constricted the road that leads to the Kingdom. And those who enter there are few.*[281] But to those who are firmly resolved to keep his holy commandments, he says, *My yoke is easy and my burden is light.*[282] Therefore it is necessary in the beginning of combat to live out the holy commandments of God with a resolute will, so that seeing our vigilance and effort, our good Lord might send us readiness of will and great joy in serving his glorious designs. For indeed, our will shall be prepared by the Lord[283] in such a way that we continuously do good with great joy. Then we will truly sense that *it is God who works in us both to desire and to work for his satisfaction.*[284]

94. Just as beeswax cannot receive the mark of a seal if it has not yet been warmed up or thoroughly softened, so it is with the human person: if he has not been tested in efforts and weaknesses, he is incapable of receiving the seal of God's virtue. Therefore the Lord says to divine Paul: *My grace is enough for you, for my power is made perfect in weakness.* And the Apostle brags of himself saying, *I would rather boast most gladly of my weaknesses, in order that the power of Christ may dwell with me.*[285] But in Proverbs, too, it is written, *for whom the Lord loves he reproves, and he chastises the son he favors.*[286] And the Apostle calls weaknesses those rebellions of the enemies of the Cross who constantly attacked him and all the saints of his time so that they would not exalt themselves, as he himself says, on account of the extraordinary nature of his revelations;[287] but rather they preserved the gift of God and persevered thanks to their humility and their striving for perfection amid so many humiliations. We on the other hand call weakness evil thought and physical maladies.

In those times, when the bodies of the saints who fought against sin were handed over to mortal blows and other types of afflic-

---

[281] Matt 7:14.
[282] Matt 11:30.
[283] See Prov 8:35.
[284] Phil 2:13.
[285] 2 Cor 12:9.
[286] Prov 3:12.
[287] See 2 Cor 12:7.

tions, they kept above the passions that invaded their human nature though sin. But now that peace has spread in the churches, thanks be to the Lord,[288] it is therefore necessary that pious warriors be tested with frequent illnesses in the body and with evil thoughts in the soul. This is so especially in those whose knowledge works with full sense and complete certitude, so that they are kept from every sort of vainglory and dissipation, and can receive in their hearts through great humility, as I mentioned, the seal of divine beauty according to what the Saint says: *the light of your face, Lord, is sealed upon us.*[289] So it is necessary to take on the will of the Lord gratefully. Then indeed the continued illnesses and the fight against diabolical thoughts will be considered our second martyrdom. Since the one who ordered the holy martyrs back then by means of impious magistrates—"Deny Christ, desire the splendors of this life"—it is he who continues to fight even today against the servants of God by continually telling them the same thing. He who used to afflict the bodies of the just and grossly abused the honorable teachers using agents who served his diabolical design, it is he who still today achieves all sorts of suffering and insults against pious confessors—above all when, for the cause of the Lord's glory, they laboriously aid the impoverished. Therefore, it is incumbent on us, with steadfastness and patience, to carry out the martyrdom of our conscience before God, for it is said, *with patience I awaited the Lord, and he came to my assistance.*[290]

95. Humble-mindedness is a difficult affair: its greatness is proportionate to the measure of perfection attained through many fights. It comes to maturity[291] in those who participate in divine knowledge in two ways. When the pious warrior is in the middle stage of the spiritual experience he comes to have a more humble

---

[288] See 1 Pet 1:2.

[289] Ps 4:7.

[290] Ps 39:2.

[291] *Paraginomai* has been translated as "be present," "come to support," (R) "comes to" (P). A valid translation of the term is also "come to maturity," which I have chosen since our author is using the context of spiritual progress and this seems most fitting.

sentiment, be it on account of his bodily weakness, or because of those groundless hatreds on account of his concern for justice, or because of evil thoughts. But when the mind is illumined by holy grace with keen sense and is full of conviction then the soul possesses humble-mindedness as if by nature. Fattened with divine goodness,[292] she cannot exalt herself with the burden of vainglory even if she continually toils at all the commandments of God. She considers herself lower than everything because she has communion with divine goodness.[293]

The first humble-mindedness often brings with it sorrow and discouragement; the second, joy but with an ever-wise[294] reserve. Therefore the first one is present in those who are in the middle stage of combat, while the other is entrusted[295] to those who approach perfection. Because of this, the first one is often scorned by those who enjoy this life's prosperity; the second one, though, even should she be offered all the kingdoms of this world,[296] doesn't flinch, nor does she feel sin's awful darts; since she is spiritual she completely ignores all bodily glory. But it is absolutely necessary that the warrior pass through the first in order to arrive at the second, since if grace does not soften up our free will beforehand through the former by way of pedagogical suffering in the form of a trial—not by obligation—the magnificence of the second will not be granted us.

96. Those who are friends of this life's pleasures proceed from thoughts to faults. Since they are carried away by indiscriminate reasoning, they desire to translate almost all their passionate ideas into lawless conversation and sacrilegious works. On the other hand, those who have committed themselves to practice the ascetical life go from faults to evil thoughts or some bad and harmful

---

[292] See Ps 62:6.

[293] *Epieikes*, lit. "concerns suitability," "fairness," "what is meet," or "reasonableness." My translation attempts to clarify this difficult text. A, F, and M translate it as "goodness." P translates this as "forebearance." R has opted for "reasonableness," which is literal but difficult to understand.

[294] Lit. "all-wise."

[295] Lit. "sent down."

[296] See Matt 4:8.

words. When demons see such people give themselves over to regaling and taunts or conversing about inanities or off-color subjects, laughing indecently, immoderately exalting themselves, or desiring vain and futile glory, of one accord they [the demons] arm themselves against them. Above all they take advantage of their love for glory and they leap at them as if through a darkened window and plunder their souls. It would be necessary then, for those who want to dwell in the abundance of virtue not to aspire to glory, nor seek the crowd or continually go out, and never make fun of others—even if they should merit it—nor seek to hold many discourses even though they speak well. In fact, many words dissipate the mind to no end, making it not only incapable of spiritual activity, but handing it over to the devil of tepidity,[297] which weakens it without measure and hands it over to the devil of sorrow, and then to the ones of anger. Therefore it is necessary that they consecrate themselves to the observance of the holy commandments and a profound memory of the Lord of glory. For *he who keeps the commandment knows no evil word,*[298] which means he will not turn aside to evil thoughts and words.

97. When the heart is struck with burning pain by the devil's bowshots, the person under attack is often under the impression that he feels real darts. The soul hates its own passions because it is still at the beginner's stage of purification; for if she did not greatly suffer the effrontery of sin, she would not be able to enjoy the goodness of righteousness so richly. Let him who wants to purify his heart fire it in the memory of the Lord Jesus in every moment, having that as his only meditation and sole occupation. For it is necessary that they who want to rid themselves of filth not pray off and on, but that they devote themselves in every moment to prayer in the custody of their mind, even should they live outside of houses of prayer. For in the same way that one who wants to purify gold, if he lets up the fire of the crucible only for an instant, the metal hardens once again. So, too, for someone

---

[297] *Akēdia*—the enemy of the friend of God. This is the bane of the religious life as discussed by all the ascetical writers. See GC 58.

[298] Eccl 8:5.

who sometimes remembers God and sometimes does not—he loses in his rest what he had gained in prayer. Proper to a person who is friendly with virtue is to consume all that is earthly in his heart through the memory of God, so that, little by little, evil is consumed by the fire of the recollection of goodness, and the soul returns perfectly to its natural shine but with an even greater splendor.

98. Impassibility[299] does not consist in not being attacked by demons, because then we would all have to depart from this world, as the Apostle says,[300] but in remaining undefeated[301] when we are attacked by them. Thus, the iron-armored warriors sustain the shots of their enemies, hear the report of the shot, and they even see almost all of the arrows shot at them, but they are undefeated when attacked thanks to the solidity of their battle armor. They are dressed for battle and trust in the iron that protects them. But as regards us, covered in the armor of the holy light, with the helmet of salvation,[302] let us destroy the dark phalanxes of demons through our good works. For sure, it is not merely our not committing evil which makes us pure, but our forceful rejection of things evil through our attention to the good.

99. When the godly person is victorious over nearly all of his passion, two demons await to fight against him. One oppresses his soul terribly, bringing her from a great love for God to indiscreet zeal to such an extent that she does not want others to please God as much as she. The other demon moves about the body with a type of burning sensation that seeks carnal union. This begins in the body because this pleasure is proper to our nature for procreation, and, therefore, one is easily overcome by it after that, as God allows. For when God sees that one of his warriors begins to flourish with a great amount of virtues, he lets him be stained by such a demon in order that he recognize himself as the vilest

[299] See GC 62.
[300] See 1 Cor 5:10.
[301] Lit. "unattacked."
[302] See Eph 6:11.

of worldly men. Indeed, this stirring up of passions occurs after good actions or even precedes them, so that through this being preceded or followed by passion, one seems somewhat useless to oneself,[303] regardless of his merits. We fight better against the first of these demons with much humility and love; and against the second we fight with self-mastery, the restraint from anger, and deep thoughts about death, so that in sensing the Holy Spirit's unceasing action, we become, in the Lord, masters of these passions.

100. Whoever from among us becomes a participant of holy knowledge will become aware of all our dissipation, even if unintentional. For Job says rightly, *you pointed out even my involuntary transgressions,*[304] and rightfully so. For if anyone does not abandon the memory of God nor neglect his holy commandments, then he will fall under neither involuntary nor voluntary faults. It is necessary therefore immediately to offer the Master an intense confession of our involuntary faults, that is to say, in practice of the usual rule (since it is impossible for a human to not fall into human faults), until our conscience should find in its tears of love a certainty that its faults are forgiven. It is said, *If we acknowledge our sins, he is faithful and just and will forgive our sins and cleanse us from every injustice.*[305] And we have constantly to cultivate the sense of confession, so that through heightening our conscience it does not deceive itself believing to have confessed to God enough, since God's judgment is much greater than our conscience, even if someone with total certainty not be aware of any fault. As wisest Paul teaches us, saying, *I do not even pass judgment on myself; I am not conscious of anything against me, but I am not thereby justified; the one who judges me is the Lord.*[306] So, if we do not sufficiently confess these faults as we ought, at the moment of our departure we will discover a dark terror within ourselves. We who love the Lord

[303] See Luke 17:10.
[304] Job 14:17.
[305] 1 John 1:9.
[306] 1 Cor 4:3-4.

should pray that we be found exempt of all fear in that moment, since he who is found in fear will not freely pass before the princes of Tartar.[307] For they reckon the cowardly soul as ally to their evil.[308] But the soul who exults in God's love at the hour of his dissolution will be borne by angels of peace above and beyond all the dark armies in battle array. For he will be lifted on the wings of spiritual love since he always bears within himself the love which is the fullness of the law.[309] Therefore, in the Lord's coming, those who find themselves having left this life with such confidence will be snatched up along with all the saints.[310] But those who fear at the moment of death, if only a little, will be left below with the multitude of all the other men submitted to judgment, to be tested by the fire of judgment,[311] and according to their actions they will receive their proper destiny from our good God and King Jesus Christ; because he is the God of justice; and the opulence and the sweetness of his kingdom is bestowed upon us who love him[312] forever and ever. Amen.

These are the ascetical treatises of Saint Diadochus, Bishop of the City of Photikē in Epiros of Iliria. One hundred chapters, two thousand and three hundred lines.

---

[307] Rulers of the netherworld.
[308] See *Homily on the Ascension*, 3.
[309] See Rom 13:10.
[310] See 1 Thess 4:16.
[311] See 1 Pet 1:7.
[312] See Ps 35:9.

Homily on the Ascension of Our Lord Jesus Christ

I. Bring me now to the Jewish[1] priests, for this is the hour for words of victory. Bring here, preacher and herald of Christ, speak and paint for us the scene with the power of your truth, how they tossed their wrong-headed silver[2] upon those soldiers,[3] thinking to hide the incomprehensible truth with their lie. And how we now, ministers of Christ, await the Lord who rose from the dead on the third day and rose up to the heavens which boast without end for having received a Savior such as this by way of a prodigy which so divinely surpassed them. The earth, sustained by his will, could no longer sustain him. A brilliant cloud took him up,[4] clearly completing the figure of prophecy. Angels with their hymns restored him to his inherited throne, chanting without pause, *the Lord of Hosts is the King of Glory*.[5] And the Psalmist, foreseeing in the Holy Spirit his ascension from earth to heaven, sang: *God mounts the throne amid shouts of joy; the Lord, amid trumpet blasts*.[6] For thus the Inspired one foresaw in song[7] the holy Gospels.

---

[1] *Ioudaioi* in John's gospel referred to those Jews living in the area of Judaea who colluded with the Roman sentencing of Christ. Diadochus might be using the term in the same vein. Further, as Jews did not permit the early Christians to be considered believers within the Jewish faith it became quite easy for the Romans to persecute the early Christians with impunity. This explains the large number of Christian martyrs in the first three centuries. This historic fact of course explains but does not justify any anti-Jewish sentiment among some early Christians.

[2] Lit. "silver of ill-advisedness."

[3] See Matt 28:12.

[4] See Acts 1:9.

[5] Ps 23:10.

[6] Ps 47:6.

[7] A follows D in translating this as "foreseeing the voice of the holy Gospels." The word *ōdē* is poetic Attic Greek for "ode" or song. I don't understand why

II. But those who boast of having most faithful Abraham for their father[8] do not want that the Savior of all should have risen from the dead—the wretches! They daily think to sully the beauty of such a truth as this with their empty rumors—*and this story has circulated among the Jews to the present day*[9]—a truth even the devils recognize. But those who profess to have received the Commandments from the Lord have decided not to honor him with their words, even when the Prophet says, *O Lord, our Lord, how wonderful is your name through all the earth! You have set your majesty above the heavens!*[10] and again, *Arise over the heavens, oh God; your glory above all the earth.*[11] This is something the sophists of evil were never able to distort, even when they subtly rationalized[12] the lie of their father,[13] since he who has been lifted and exalted above the heavens is most certainly the Lord of all, he who first descended to earth and rose to the heavens. Therefore in another place the Prophet foretold this saying, *Lord, incline your heavens and come; touch the mountains and make them smoke. Flash forth lightning and scatter them.*[14] He said this to foretell to those who were yet seated in the shadows of death the defeat of hell's powers, a ruin of which we are convinced by many proofs, that was brought about by the burial and resurrection of the Lord. Furthermore, in another chapter we have the Psalmist who says, *rising to a lofty height, he took captivity captive, and distributed gifts among men.*[15] By means of his resurrection the only begotten Son took humanity from the captivity of death, and rising above the highest heavens he prepared weapons for those who love justice—for he is the

---

they chose the word "voice" since one does not foresee a voice. But since our Author has just quoted the Psalmist it seems only logical that the prophecy is "in song" as I have translated this passage.

  [8] See John 8:33.
  [9] Matt 28:15.
  [10] Ps 8:2.
  [11] Ps 56:6.
  [12] Lit. "philosophized."
  [13] See John 8:44.
  [14] Ps 144:5-6.
  [15] Ps 68:19.

King of glory—securing[16] the spiritual armor each day of those whom he recruits under the badge of humility. For it was fitting that he restore praise from the mouths of babes and infants,[17] but reject once and for all those who, in their presumption, think themselves perfect. For the true seal of piety is humility. According to the prophecy, therefore, those who refuse to be convinced that through the resurrection of Christ we dwell in the light of the living will receive the fruits of their folly.

III. But we, my brothers, let us contemplate the words of the Psalmist once again to see anew with the eyes of the Lord who rose up to the heavens on a cloud. Reason invites me to silence for a moment the testimony of the apostles so as not to seem to the ignorant that I am my own advocate, since every apostolic word is witnessed to by prophetic truth,[18] given that their discourses are recognized as the products prophetic oracles. Thus, what the prophets hinted at through their prescience with regard to the Incarnation of the Lord, this the apostles clearly revealed through their knowledge under inspiration of the Holy Spirit. *In the course of the years you will be made manifest; when the time comes you will be recognized.*[19] Let us say further, *O Lord, our Lord, how wonderful is your name through all the earth! You have set your majesty above the heavens*[20] in order that we might clearly know that the incarnation of the Lord and his ascension from earth to heaven, whose memory we celebrate today, filled the earth with knowledge of God. When he was on earth the majority understood but very little of the grandeur of his glory. But since he visibly ascended into heaven, fulfilling the will of the Father, as was fitting, all creation was replete with admiration and knowledge, contemplating the

---

[16] A and D chose to translate this "strengthen" or "fortify," which does not seem to make logical sense, since armor is secured when put on, not strengthened.

[17] See Ps 8:3.

[18] See 1 Pet 1:19.

[19] Hab 3:2.

[20] Ps 8:2.

Lord of all things ascending and being accepted. He was raised or exalted above all the heavens, according to the prophecy, in as much a he was man; but in as much as he was God, *God ascends amid shouts of joy, with trumpet blasts.*[21]

IV. The Prophet would not have used these expressions if he had not first seen with his own eyes—and that without error—his descent. How could it otherwise have been logical to say, *Arise over the heavens, oh God, and your glory over the earth*, and further, *God arose amid shouts of joy*, if the theologian had not first seen his descent and ascent, with the help of the Holy Spirit? Therefore, as I have already said, in certain parts it affirms that he was lifted up, and in others that he ascended, so that we might believe that the Lord himself is God and man in one Person. Through divinity he ascended; through his Body, as it is said, he was lifted up, that is, assumed. So, for all of this, we have to think that he who descends is the same as he who ascends above all the heavens,[22] so as to fill everything with his goodness and, having first rescued his apostles from the passions of sin through the descent of the Holy Spirit, he exalted them once and for all. Why else would it say, *Arise over the heavens, oh God; and your glory above all the earth; so that your beloved be saved?*[23] For truly they are the beloved of the Lord, in the first place, who, having shared his passion in everything, became eyewitnesses and heralds of his magnificence.

V. In this way it is one and the same Lord whom the prophets announced, although the manner of his incarnation they did not confuse into only one nature, as some hold today. Rather, they foretold divinely those aspects that corresponded to his divinity and humanly those aspects that corresponded to his body, in order clearly to teach that the Lord who arose or was lifted to the heavens, such as he is, is from the Father; and he who came into being from the Virgin remains man, being one in form[24] and one in

---

[21] Ps 47:6.
[22] See Eph 4:10.
[23] Ps 56:6; 59:7.
[24] *Eidos.*

Personhood. He who was incorporeal having taken a form[25] upon assuming flesh, ascended visibly, therefore, to that place from which he invisibly descended and was incarnated. Thus he was assumed into glory,[26] was believed in on account of his power, and is anticipated in fear, as we await that prophetic cloud which will serve him once again in his descent. For, as the prophets foretold, then the cloud would serve him when it appears once again as a corporeal but light substance bearing the Lord robed in a body. For, as I said, as God he sustains all that is, but as man, he will be sustained by a cloud, so that the friend of souls defies the laws of the nature he assumed.

VI. Therefore, divine Paul prophetically taught us that the saints, too, will be taken up above the clouds when the Lord arrives, and that he is expected to come upon a cloud.[27] For what is fitting for the incarnate God's body is also fitting for those he will divinize through the abundance of his grace, because it pleases God to make gods of humans. Let it not be held, my brothers, that the density of human nature in which the Word of God was known substantially to participate has modified the truth of each of the natures that exist in him invisibly through the splendor of divine and glorious substance. For the glorious God did not take flesh in order to appear one of his own creatures, but rather in order to destroy forever, through participation in our nature, the habit of mind sown in it through the serpent. In this way it is a habit, not a nature, that the incarnation of the Word modified, so that we might be stripped of the memory of evil and robed in the charity of God: not transformed into what we were not, but renewed through glory by the transformation into what we were. Glory and power to Him who descended invisibly from the heavens and visibly ascended—to Him who is before all ages, now and forever, age after age. Amen.

---

[25] *Eidopoieō.*
[26] See 1 Tim 3:16.
[27] See 1 Thess 4:17.

The Vision of
Saint Diadochus,
Bishop of Photikē
in Epiros

1. Question: Why did you hold the desert in such high esteem? Tell me, I beg you—so I asked wise John one night as if he were present, my soul all serene. And you, glorious Mother Church, why—I said once again—why did you have such fervor for this shabby wild man? And that voice that delights men's ears, why did you so joyfully acclaim him in the desert waste? And he—or better said, as if it were he truly present to me—conversed with these words.

Response: How could I speak to you, friend, if I am outside of this passing age and you live in it as long as God wants?

2.   Q.   You could—I said—admirable man, if you want to let me see your passion for wisdom, by way of questions and answers. And if you so desire, I will determine the order once we come to the area of subjects so that you teach and I learn. Why did you rejoice in the desert, courageous man, and found a city of virtues there[1] with your preaching and life?

R.   The footsteps[2] of a pure life—he said—the fragrance of the desert, the escape[3] from customs of the city, the pleasant converse of the silence of this place; that is why I persevered there undoing the storm of human thoughts through the strength of endurance, awaiting in spirit the word whose voice you have evoked.[4]

---

[1] A follows D making this "here below" while the word actually means "in that place."

[2] Again the image of following footsteps of the invisible Lover. Cf. Definition 3.

[3] A translates this as "liberation from," thus missing the idea of *fuga mundi* so prevalent among the desert fathers.

[4] John is the voice; Christ is the Word.

3. Q. Fine. What form does this voice take? This is what I have been longing to learn from you.

R. It speaks—he said—of Israel's superficiality, since it was they who sealed their ears with the wax of insolence, rejecting the resonance of the Most High's knowledge. I called out from the desert places to the savage peoples to come to the encounter of faith,[5] which clearly takes the form of the enigma of contemplation.

4. Q. But—I said—who was it that revealed the power of what is preached?

R. The Word of the Father uttered in the Spirit.

5. Q. Certainly. But tell me, how did you recognize whom you did not know?

R. By seeing a divine power in human form.

6. Q. As far as I am concerned, divine man, I admire your daring.

R. With regard to what?

7. Q. Because being merely human you baptized the Son of God.

R. I overcame daring by obedience, since nothing is more humble than obedience.

8. Q. Most assuredly. From a broken[6] heart is obedience engendered.

R. You have spoken well.

9. Q. I, once again: How did you recognize the Holy Spirit's beatitude as it descended from the heavens in a form upon the Lord? For you give witness to having seen it under the form of a dove.

---

[5] A adds *de Dios* ("of God"), while D adds *divine*.
[6] Lit. "ground down" or "crushed."

R.   There was a joyful breeze which preceded his ineffable presence, and then the voice which resounded from the sky immediately afterward, indicating as if by a finger the Son witnessed to by the Father—this showed me clearly the infinitude of that dove.

10. Q.   Very well. But the voice that rang out, was it the Father's or was it from a power shouting on God's behalf?
    R.   It was the Father's.

11. Q.   And how, tell me, could he have the sense of speech,[7] if his nature is incorporeal and invisible?
    R.   The Divine One does not speak by way of vocal chords, but when his will wants to make something heard, this will impinge upon one who is chosen like a voice that speaks by way of divine operation. Thus those hear whom he wants to hear, even if those who are meant to hear are in the same place as others who are unworthy of hearing. Thus the voice was heard in that place only where the Lord was baptized. If it were not that way, the whole world would have heard that thunderous voice, even if it were to come from an angel. For those who desire, it is possible to inquire in the Gospel, above all that of divine Mark, who remembers the voice that rang out over the mountain when the Lord was transfigured. He says, *Then a cloud came, throwing a shadow over them; and from the cloud came a voice, "This is my beloved Son. Listen to him."*[8]

12. Q.   You have instructed me well. And the Holy and Life-giving Spirit who was seen under a form, how should we interpret that, for he is eternal and immutable, as you have said? Therefore, what form does the blessed nature have?
    R.   Here too it is fitting that one marvel at the contemplation of the Father's voice, for the invisible and immutable nature of the Spirit was not transformed into the form of a dove simply

[7] Lit. "sensed voice."
[8] Mark 9:7-8.

because he wanted to be seen; rather, he who was made worthy of such beauty saw that which the divine Spirit made visible to man when he descended from heaven. And so it was such that by his will the form was visible for him to contemplate yet without anyone being able to say that he saw the ineffable and inconceivable nature transformed and confined to this form, as if by contraction. For in the same way, the prophets saw God as in the vision of a form. He did not reveal himself changed into a figure, rather they were made to see the formless One in the form of glory, showing himself to them in the form of his choosing, not of his nature. It is an act of his will that clearly reveals to them the form of visions of glory, since he wanted to let himself be seen in a form entirely of his choosing.

13. Q. How then will God be seen by humans in the incorruptible age?

R. The incorruptibility of the body, according to the true expression, makes a person close to God. And so God will be seen by humans as man, as such, can see God.

14. Q. So, as a figure then?

R. No, but in virtue of glory. That is why those who will be judged worthy of it will be constantly in the light, rejoicing in the glory of God's love, but unable to comprehend what the nature of God's light is that illumines them. In the same way, therefore, that God can limit himself where he will, remaining nonetheless unlimited, so too he is seen where he desires while remaining invisible.

15. Q. What are we to understand by God's virtue?

R. Beauty without form, known only in glory.

16. Q. For me, humanly thinking, glory is perceived as an extraordinary vision.

R. Don't think that way. Beauty of this immaterial and blessed nature, according to the faith, is superior to all forms on account of its great purity. Therefore, God sees as present those things that do not yet exist.[9] For if that ineffable nature were in a form, it would not be able to contemplate as existing that which did not yet exist.

17. Q. What do you mean?

R. I mean that whatever is in a form cannot know beforehand what will be said or will occur, because it is completely limited in its nature. This would be the case even if it had vision as the totality of its nature. Thus while our intellect by some rich eye takes in everything but cannot know anything of what is going to happen, even after the soul leaves the body; so it is believed that the soul will then be like an eye—and it is reasonable to think the same way about the heavenly powers whose entire nature is considered really to be vision.

18. Q. Why do some hold that these [powers] and the soul are beyond[10] form?

R. Such conjectures are far from reasonable. Given that neither angels nor the soul can be seen, we ought to think, according to unanimous opinion, that they are living beings without figure. But we must hold that they have vision, they have beauty and spiritual limits, to such an extent that the splendor of their thoughts is their form and beauty. Therefore, when the soul has beautiful thoughts it is illuminated and visible everywhere. But when it has evil thoughts it is dim and left without anything to admire. Just when the shadows are apprehended by the pupil thanks to its deep and keen clarity—something we ought to call the power of sense sight—(it is fitting that we treat this theme as much as possible with a visible example), they appear as forms of its operation, so too, when the mind, from its own passion, seizes a thought, [the thought] becomes like a form of the soul's

---

[9] D's translation is confusing: *Dieu seul domine comme present ce qui n'est pas encore*: "God only dominates as present those things that do not exist."

[10] Both A and D translate *huper* as "superior" but "beyond" seems more fitting since the question is not simply about the qualities of souls and heavenly powers but about their nature.

operation, which it is in all its subtlety. For what the operation achieves in the case of immaterial natures, this it becomes, as I mentioned, whether this occurs in glory or in suffering. This is what we have to think about the apostate angels. While they had sentiments proper to angels, the very beauty of their thoughts became for them the form of their glory; but when they despised the thoughts loved by God, they made of their joy a form of dishonor.

19. Q.   And so, in contrast to the density of our bodies, we have to call angels and the soul living beings without matter or form; but when speaking of divine purity, does there not seem to be more to it?

R.   The form is the end product of every beginning. But it is believed that the beauty of the Eternal One, who alone has no beginning, is above every form, since he is not the end product of a beginning but has being from himself in the supra-natural nature.

20. Q.   Explain to me this one, too, I said, wanting to know more about this. Why, with regard to God, do we speak of beauty but not of form? For undoubtedly it is in the form that beauty is admired.

R.   Because the beauty of God's glory is his nature.

21. Q.   Then what can be said to what the Psalmist mentions: *I will appear in justice in your presence. I will be satisfied when I see your glory.*[11]

R.   This was said by the prophet, but not as if the divine nature had a face or were a figure; rather, it is that in the form and glory of the Son, the Father, who is formless, will reveal himself to us. Therefore, God was pleased that his Word was incarnated in human form, retaining—how could it be otherwise?—his omnipotent glory, so that a human being, upon beholding the density

[11] Ps 17:15.

of the figure of this glorious flesh (given that a form can see form), after it has been purified by the resurrection, might be able to see its beauty, as it were [looking] upon God. In this inscrutable way the Father will reveal himself to the just as he manifests himself to angels, while the Son will be readily visible because he has a body. It is truly fitting then, that they who are to be knowingly ruled by God for eternity should behold their Sovereign in every moment, something that would have been impossible if the God-Word had not taken form upon himself, becoming man.

22. Q.   Through faith and reason you have taught [me], oh Word, fully revealing to me John's pillar.[12] But now, I beg you, finish explaining to me angelic contemplation. This is similar, I suppose, to the condition of the soul after the resurrection.

R.   What, then? Speak.

23. Q.   Do angels have sense or not?

R.   According to the discourse on knowledge it was theirs to choose their "sense"[13] by virtue of their freedom. Thus some of them submitted to passion and fell. On the other hand, since those who did not permit themselves to be seduced by apostasy kept themselves innocent and impassible by professing the glorious and divine Spirit, they are also above all senses, enjoying immutable glory. Hence they also always have like thoughts.[14] For not only do they know beauty in a similar way, they are similarly unaware of all that is contrary to it. And this is what the just can expect upon reaching the resurrection, when the fruit of their free acts is presented to God in perfect submission.[15]

---

[12] D sees in this word a reference to the pillar from Exodus that led the people of God through the desert, thus linking that liberation to the liberation from sin wrought by John's baptism.

[13] *Aisthēsis*: something of an anomaly here, expressed with a volitional quality not common to Diadochus's usage of the term. Most likely our author refers to "sense" as the fruit of previous choices, something attained and honed.

[14] Here we have an example of angelic discernment of their own spirits.

[15] See 1 Cor 15:27-28.

24. Q. Well said, but do those holy and heavenly powers sing hymns with a voice or, as some purport, with an interior word?
R. With their voice. For if we profess that they are like flames of fire, as the Scriptures hold,[16] it is evident that they must sing to God with a most excellent voice.[17] Therefore many saints often perceive their voices in visions, as the Scriptures indicate.

25. Q. That is clear. But some will maintain with equal force that the word from an angelic voice ought to be understood according to the explanation given about the divine voice.
R. Since all things are possible for God,[18] he reveals himself by speaking whenever he wants, but keeps himself above all things because only he is immaterial. But it is impossible for angels to do. Because they do not speak, if they could manifest themselves by speech whenever they desired they might also be able to create from nothing if they should so choose!

26. Q. Very well. But what must we think about the soul separated from the body?
R. The soul separated from the body, until it returns to take the body through the resurrection, sings to God by way of the interior word, as is fitting for it, given that the faculty of speech is received from the body alone. On the other hand, given that angels were created with a simple and vibrant nature, they use, as we have already mentioned, incessant voices. It is not so much that they express themselves by way of a corporeal organ, but have a type of extraordinary and continuous mobility which is of the order of speech. Their ethereal nature lends itself to chant and impels them to break out in unceasing and pristine praise.

---

[16] See Heb 1:7.

[17] Diadochus seems to be indicating that such qualities attributed to angels are more metaphorical than positive. He is referring to Ps 103:4, which compares angels to fire and wind.

[18] See Matt 19:26.

27. Q. This is clear. But what are we to make of how they take a form when they are sent by God to some saints?

R. This question is out of place in this lesson and [should] forfeit a response. Nonetheless, we have to say that they are sent by God, consider what form to take, and immediately enter into it through their imagination. In virtue of their lithe nature, they submit themselves[19] to their desire as if condensed by the sheer force of will and go from invisible to visible without any hindrance, regardless of what it may be. As I said, they show themselves in whatever form they choose but only to the pure and spiritual soul. For it is proper to the pure and spiritual soul consciously to see the form that imagination presents to it. So if what we call the imagination does not find the correct dispositions in that to which it appears, it cannot produce the contact in a visible way between angel and man. Therefore, as it would seem to me, they use a sensible voice and the voice imitates, for the reason already stated, the figure that the imagination [presents].

28. Q. That is convincing. But I beg you, O Master Word, explain to me before the day comes—for I know that when it comes you will immediately depart, for you cannot bear to be present to the soul to speak with it any longer or see the winged forms of life— tell me if angels sent by God to earth, during their time on earth, must abandon their dwelling place in heaven.

R. It is impossible for them to remain as they are in heaven above so long as they are on the earth. This is proper alone to the Word of God made man, who manifests himself on the earth without being purely imaginative while not abandoning the heavenly regions, and yet retaining all of his uncircumscribed nature. We should recognize that wherever there are angelic powers, they see everything above the heavens just as they do the things of this world, as if they were right in front of them. Their transparent nature and the fact that they have a sort of universal vision is primarily merited by grace of the Holy Spirit. But only God sees

---

[19] Lit. submit their nature.

the future up close, because he is above all and through his glory contains as present not only that which is, but also what which will come to be. Therefore only he knows even the (hidden) intentions of the heart.

29. Q.   So then the separated soul, according to the explanation given on angels, does not see as if in a mirror only the regions of incorporeal beings, but sees in a similar way everything that is in the world?

R.   By no means. Since angels were created at once with a simple nature they can see not only what is above space but what is in space, too. For it is proper to the sublime nature to not be seen by those in a dense nature, but to see that nature in its entirety. But the soul, once it is separated from the body, cannot see what is in space: *The Spirit sweeps over us and we are gone; our place knows us no more.*[20] Given that it is in virtue of its union with the body which puts it in space, once separated from the body it can no longer see—necessarily—what the body saw previously. For humans have their integrity in composition; the angels, on the other hand, have theirs in the simplicity of their nature.

Only these things of John's wisdom, and perhaps some other thing, the Word made manifest and revealed to me, O illustrious and many crowned King.[21] For when day came he was gone, leaving me still thirsting for his friendship.

---

[20] Ps 103:16.
[21] The title of the King of Byzantium.

The Catechesis of Diadochus Himself: Questions and Responses

1. Question: What was in the world before it came into being?
   Response: God who made the world.

2. Q. If the world did not yet exist how was he in the world?
   R. Because, even before it came into being, it was completely in God as if it had already come into being. So, too, humans who have not yet been introduced into the world are already in God as if they had come into being. Thus, in effect, all beings subsist in him, even those that have not yet been created, even if we have never even conceived of them.

3. Q. If it is as you claim, that God was in the world before the world came into being through him, what did God become when he created the world? Could it be that he separated himself from the world? Or is he still in the world?
   R. Spatially, God who made them has not distanced himself from his works. Where could he go to, he who is omnipresent and fills everything with His divinity? But he is above every nature and their properties and is separate from it all through his immensity and incomprehensibility.

4. Q. How, not being locally distanced from his works, but remaining omnipresent, as you put it, is he separated from all things?
   R. The question is difficult to conceive, even if it is not so difficult to formulate—but nothing is impossible for God.[1] And

---

[1] See Matt 19:26.

in virtue of this he is able to satisfy you regarding this, too. Listen then with attention. Our human intellect is not contained by walls or spatially limited, even if all the while the body is enclosed in a room and tied down with bonds; the mind is outside and wanders freely wherever it pleases, without separating itself from the body or leaving the house: it is with them even when it leaves them, and separates itself while remaining united with them. So, too, God is everywhere and in everything and yet outside of it all. He is nowhere with regard to his nature, his essence, his glory, for he is uncircumscribed.

5.   Q.   How does the Uncircumscribed fill all things? And he who fills all things, how is he uncircumscribed and yet not in any place?

R.   God, according to unanimous opinion, is everywhere and fills all things. Nevertheless he is not integrally mixed in with visible things, rather separate from them just as we have said; and he is not in any place in any way in which we can understand, for nobody—not even the angels—knows where God is. If you hear that they are before him, it is better to say that they are before the throne of his glory and not having the strength to look at the splendor that emanates from him, in their fear they cover their faces stupefied, and raise a divine hymn unable to silence it. Trembling before his unbearable glory, they cannot even conceive or consider where the Lord is or what he is like. If they, then, lack the fortitude to fix their gaze on his brilliant radiance, how then could they extend their curiosity beyond that? That God exists and is everywhere and fills all things, the angels and the saints who have been purified well know, for they have been illumined and enlightened by the Holy Spirit. But where he is, what he is like, what he is, none of those beings knows, except the Father [who knows] the Son, and the Son [who knows] the Father, and the Holy Spirit who [knows] the Father and the Son, for it is co-eternal and consubstantial with them. These three, as One, know themselves and are known by one another, as he who is God by nature and Son of God says: *No one knows what pertains to man except the spirit of man that dwells in him, so too, no one knows what pertains to God except the Spirit of God,*[2] and again, *No one knows the Father except the Son, and no one knows the Son except the Father and anyone to whom the Son wishes to reveal him.*[3]

6.   Q.   How does Christ say, *"See that you do not despise one of these little ones, for I say to you that their angels in heaven always look upon the face of my heavenly Father."*[4] And further, *Blessed are the clean of heart, for they will see God,*[5] while you, on the other hand, say that angels do not know what and where God is?

R.   Just as at midday with the sun shining, we clearly contemplate the light emanating from it, but we lack all fortitude to look at it, to contemplate it, to observe it, and nonetheless, we say at the same time that we do see it; so too, the angels and the saints contemplating his glory resplendent from the Spirit, see in it the Father and the Son. But the sinners and the impure do not. They are like blind people and those deprived of all their senses. Like blind people who do not see the light of the sensible sun shining, so neither do these contemplate the divine light that shines forever, nor do they feel his warmth.

7.   Q.   What do those who are purified in heart and mind see?

R.   Since God is light, and supreme light at that, those who see him see nothing more than light. And this is evident from those who saw Christ's face resplendent like the sun and his clothing which became like light;[6] and the Apostle Paul, seeing God-Light converted to knowledge of God;[7] and a myriad of other saints.

---

[2] 1 Cor 2:11.
[3] Matt 11:27-28.
[4] Matt 18:10.
[5] Matt 5:8.
[6] See Matt 17:2.
[7] See 2 Cor 4:6.

8.   Q.   How is it that God who is eternal and resplendent light is not visible to all?

R.   Because God ordained it so from the beginning, so that darkness might not have any communion with the light,[8] nor the evil or impure with the holy and pure. Therefore our sins too, like a great abyss and wall, separate us from God.[9] Moreover, our evil thoughts and vain intentions become like a high wall, separating us from the light and true life, for God is light and life. All who are deprived of him are dead in their souls; they are co-heirs and co-participants of eternal fire and darkness.

9.   Q.   Is salvation not attainable for those who have not reached such a degree?

R.   Since the Lord says, *there are many rooms in my Father's house,*[10] it is evident that there are many ways to salvation. But all are perfected in the one way of conversion, that is, by way of abstaining from evil, be it through the fulfillment of alms, living like a sojourner, or completing every other good work to attain the highest gifts.

---

[8] See 2 Cor 6:14.
[9] See Isa 59:2; Luke 16:26.
[10] John 14:2.

Bibliography

Argárate, Pablo. *Diadoco de Fótice: Obras Completas*. Madrid: Editorial Ciudad Nueva, Biblioteca de Patrística, 1999.

Danielou, Jean. *Bibbia e liturgia*. *La teologia biblica dei sacramenti e delle feste secondo i Padri della Chiesa*. Milan: Vita e Pensiero, 1958, 255.

Des Places, Eduoárd. *Diadoque de Photicé: Oeuvres spirituelle*, introduction, texte critique, traduction et notes. Vol. 5. Paris: Sources Chrétienne, 1966.

————. "Un père grec du V siecle, Diadoque de Photicé." *Revue d'Etudes Anciennes* 44 (1943): 61–80.

————. "Diadoco di Foticea." in *Enciclopedia Cattolica*. Vol. 4, 591–95. Rome, 1950 coll.

————. "Une catéchèse inédite de Diadoque de Photicé?" in *Recherches de Science Religieuse* 40 (1952): 129–38.

————. "La tradition manuscrite des Cent Chapitres de Diadoque de Photicé," in *Revue des Etudes Grecques* 71 (1957): 376–86.

————. "Diadoque de Photicé et le Messalianisme," in *Kyriakon Festschrift für J. Quasten* 2, 591–95. Münster: Aschendorf Verlag, 1970.

Dörr, Friedrich. *Diadochus von Photike und die Messalianer: Ein Kampf zwischen wahrer und falscher Mystik in fünften Jahrundert*. Freiburg: Herder & Co., 1937.

Dörries, Heinrich. "Diadochus und Symeon: Das Verhältnis der kephalaia gnostica zum Messalianismus." *Wort und Stunde* 1 (Göttingen, 1966): 352–422.

Frank, Karl Suso. *Gespür für Gott: Hundert Kapitel über die christliche Vollkommenheit.* Einsiedlen: Johannes Verlag, 1982.

Gribmont, Jean. "Le monachisme au IV siecle en Asie Mineure: de Gangres au Messalianisme." *Studia Patristica* 2 (1948): 400–415.

Hausherr, Irenee. "L'erreur fondamentale et la logique de Messalianisme." *Orientalia Christiana Periodica* 1 (1935): 328–60.

———. "Le grands courants de la spiritualité orientale," *Orientalia Christiana Periodica* 1 (1935):114–38.

———. *The Name of Jesus.* CS 44. Kalamazoo, MI: Cistercian Press, 1978.

Henry, Rene. "La Bibliotéque de Photius." *Analecta Bollandiana* 81 (1963): 414–17.

Hester, David. "Diadochos of Photike: The Memory and Its Purification." *Studia Patristica* 23 (1989): 49–52.

Horn, Gabriel. "Sens de l'esprit d'apres Diadoue de Photicé." *Revue d'Ascetique et de Mystique* 8 (1927): 402–19.

Krivocheine, Basil. "The Writing of St. Symeon the New Theologian." *Orientalia Christiana Periodica* 20 (1954): 324–27

Leclercq, Jean. "Culte liturgique et prière intime dans le monachisme au Moyen-age." *Maison Dieu* 69, no. 44 (1962).

Leonardi Claudio. "Alle origini della cristianità medievale: Giovanni Cassiano e Salviano di Marsiglia." *Studi Medievale* 18 (1977): 1057–1174.

Madden, Nicholas. "Aisthēsis noera (Diadochus-Maximus)." *Studia Patristica* 23 (1989): 53–60.

Marrou, Henri-Ireneé. "Diadoque de Photiké et Victor de Vita," *Revue des Études anciennes* 45 (1943): 225–32.

———. "Diadoque de Photicé et Victor de Vita," *Christiana Tempora* (Rome: Collection de l'École française de Rome,1978): 373–80.

Messana, Vincenzo. *Cento Considerazioni sulla Fede.* Rome: Cittá Nuova, 1978.

———. "Diadoco di Fotica e la cultura cristiana in Epiro nel V secolo." *Augustinianum* 19 (1979): 151–66.

———. "La nudité d'Adam et Eve chez Diadoque." *Studia Patristica* 17 (1982): 325–32.

———. "Lo Spirito santo e l'accezione clementina di senso spirituale." *Augustinianum* 20 (1980): 485–97.

———. "La chiesa orante nella catechesi spirituale di Evagrio Pontico," in *Ecclesiologia e catechesi patristica*, ed. Sergio Felici, 173–286. Roma: Pontificia Universita Salesiana, 1982.

———. "Povertà e lavoro nella paideia ascetica di Giovanni Cassiano," in *Cultura e Lingue classiche* 3, ed., Biaggio Amata. Roma: Pontifica Universita Salesiana, 1985.

———. "La *mesòtes* nel *De voluntaria paupertate* di Nilo d'Ancira." *Studia Patristica* 20 (1989): 274–82.

Morard Francois. "Monachòs, moine. Histoire du terme grec jusqu'au IV° siecle. Influences biblique et gnostique," in *Freiburger Zeitschrift fuer Philosophie und Theologie* 20 (1973): 117–36.

Pellegrino, Michele. "Un antico maestro della carità." *Studium* 53 (1956): 489–94.

Polyzogopoulos, Theodoritus. "The Life and Writings of Diadochus of Photice." *Theologia*, 55 (1984): 772–800; 1071–1101; 56 (1985): 174–221.

Randle, Guillermo. *La ciencia del espíritu—Adiestramiento integral para acompañantes espirituales.* Buenos Aires: San Benito, 2006.

Riggi, Carlo. "Il movimento messaliano da Epifanio di Salamina a Diadoco di Fotica," in *Annali della Facoltà di Lettere e Filosofia dell'Università di Cagliari*, 6, Cagliari (1987): 183–205.

Rothenhäusler, "La doctrine de la *Theologie* chez Diadoque de Photicé." *Irénikon* 14 (1937): 536–53.

———. "Zur asketischen Lehrshcrift des Diadochus von Photike." *Dia heilige Überlieferung* (1938): 86–95.

Rutherford, Janet. *One Hundred Practical Texts of Perception and Spiritual Discernment from Diadochos of Photike.* Belfast: Belfast Byzantine Texts and Translations, Institute of Byzantine Studies, 8, 2000.

Spidlík, Tomas. "L'ascesi nella chiesa orientale," in *Ascesi Cristiana*, ed., Emilio Ancilli, 163–81. Rome: Istituto Pontificio di Spiritualità Teresianum, 1977.

Spidlík, Tomas, and Innocenzo Gargano. *La spiritualità dei Padri greci oriental.* Storia della spiritualità, 3/A. Roma: Borla, 1983.

Triantaphyllopoulos, Demetrios. "He mesaionike Photike kai he these tes sten Palai Epeiro." *Actes du Xe Congrés International d´Archéologie Chrétienne* 2 (1984): 577–85.

Ware, Kallistos. "Diadochus von Photike," in *Theologische-Realenzyclopädie*, 8, 617–20. Berlin: 1981.

Zwitek, Georg. "Discretio Spirituum." *Theologie und Philosophie* 47 (1972): 36–54.

Index